Achieving Profitable Growth - Establishing the Four Points of Control

Contents

Introduction to Financial Control

Part One - The Concepts

Part Two - Techniques & Processes

Chapter 1 - Introduction

What's the Point?

So what is the purpose of this book?

I wrote it after working for over twenty years in commercial finance, starting out as an Accounts Assistant in a huge global travel company and ending up as a Finance Director of an SME in the oil and gas engineering sector. These two particular vocations both lasted around a year, which became a theme throughout my career. The longest I spent in one place was just under five years, which was somewhat unusual.

The reason for this nomadic progression was my constant yearning to fix problems. I was never really happy in a stable environment, instead preferring to go where I felt I was needed. Seems presumptuous to think I was 'needed' anywhere, I realise that, but it turns out I was right. I've always thrived in chaotic environments and over time I developed a track record for eradicating it, to the extent that I was eventually sought out by employers who needed to eradicate their own version of chaos.

In one of my last roles before I launched my own consultancy, I was appointed as Head of Finance at a relatively young company. They were having problems with their Finance Director and had decided to make a change. The FD was 'removed' and I was ushered in to bring about that change. Unfortunately it was too late. The damage had been done and there wasn't enough time to turn things around. The bank appointed administrators, turned off the cash tap and that was that. Eighty five people laid off, a few weeks before Christmas. As is often the case, they were not paid, even for the hours they had already worked that month. They would have eventually received what they were owed (or at least some of it) from the Redundancy Payments Service, several months into the new year, but it would have been a pretty lean Christmas.

The tragedy here wasn't that the company failed, although of course that is tragic in its own right. The real shame was that it could have been avoided if Financial Controls had been in place and the board had taken their accountability seriously. As I stood in the office that day, listening to the bank-appointed administrators explain to my devastated colleagues how to go about claiming their pay from the government, this book was born.

My framework - The Four Points of Control - was already in existence at that point. I had developed it several years earlier and it was my way of quickly establishing areas of concern and focal points whenever I joined a new company. It has been honed over the years and will probably never be completely perfect. Just as I am constantly learning, even at this stage of my career, the framework will continually be amended and polished, so that I can achieve better results for my clients.

So that's the point. I want to reach as many businesses as possible and instil the Four Points of Control deep in their culture and consciousness. If I can do that, I just might save a few from the same fate.

Establish Control

To properly establish and maintain Financial Control of a business is no easy task. As with anything worthwhile, the preparation and hard work can be painstaking, but it's worth it.

As you will read in this book, the odds are against you when you start a business, even if it might not seem that way in year one. The '20/60 Rule' (see Chapter 3) puts paid to many businesses after they survive and seem to thrive in their first year. Establishing control early on gives you the stability and consistency to excel in year one and then push for profitable growth from that point.

The book is structured in two parts:

Part One - The Concepts
Part Two - The Processes

In Part One, we will set out the concepts and conditions which are necessary, even vital, to the development of Financial Control. Understanding these concepts is vital to the competent execution of the processes outlined in Part Two, so if you need to read it twice to make sure it sinks in, please do so.

You probably won't need to read it twice, as the concepts are pretty logical. However, you may need to review it at a later date, or refer back to it for training purposes, so I have laid out the chapters in a way that will help you to do that.

First things first - a brief glossary of terms.

FD - Finance Director - I use this term to mean CFO, FD, Financial Controller, Finance Manager, Bean Counter or whichever role has overall responsibility for the finances of the business. In many SMEs there are no Finance staff at all and the person responsible for Finance is the same person responsible for Purchasing, Sales, Marketing or even sweeping the floor. In those cases, I mean that person. If no one within the business has this responsibility, presumably there is an external accountant, so that's who I'm talking about.

MD - Managing Director - Again, this could be any of the following: Owner, Partner, Founder, CEO, MD, Bossman or any other title which has ultimate accountability for the business.

SME - In the UK this is an acronym which stands for Small and Medium-sized Enterprises. There are criteria set out as to what constitutes different sizes of business in terms of number of employees, turnover and net worth.

Blue chip - This was originally a poker term but in the UK has come to mean a large commercial, corporate organisations, with massive sales revenues and thousands of employees.

This book is aimed squarely at SMEs, small businesses and start-ups, so large organisations will not get much of a mention, but when I do mention them, I will call them 'Blue chips'.

Accounting knowledge

You don't need to be an accountant to understand the concepts or processes outlined in this book and this is not an accounting text book. However, there are three essential accounting concepts I believe all senior managers and owners of businesses should understand. These concepts are explored and explained in Chapter 6. In terms of accounting terminology, I will need to distinguish between different types of financial statements. When I do this I will use the terms below:

Statutory Accounts: The official financial statements produced at the end of the financial year, often by an external accountant. These accounts are held and published by Companies House, a government agency, and are freely available for anyone to download.

Management Accounts: Internal financial statements produced monthly and evaluated by the senior management of an organisation for decision-making purposes. These are held internally and not disclosed or published to external parties.

Financial Reporting: All other documents used for financial analysis, whether in support of the accounts or produced/reviewed independently.

My Audience

As mentioned above, this book is aimed predominantly at SMEs and small businesses. There are good reasons for this, which are explored further throughout the book. In summary, the reason is that a large corporation has already been through the growing pains and challenges most SMEs face and has 'made it' to the other side. Generally-speaking, although they suffer from their own problems, such as a lack of agility and tighter regulation, they also enjoy advantages like economies of scale and more abundant resources. Although the Four Points of Control framework is equally valid in a large or small business, most large businesses will have established a considerable level of control (either by accident or by design) in order to become large businesses, so the advice and guidance in this book is less relevant to them.

What the Hell do I Know?

You may wonder what qualifies me to tell you anything about Financial Control. I often think the same thing when I read books like this, so I have outlined my specific experience in this introduction. Accounting and finance is one of those areas in which everyone (especially those in business) think they have some innate knowledge. It's also an area riddled with myths and misinformation. I don't claim to know everything, but I do know what good and bad look like, because I've seen both. Many times.

Many Finance professionals have a particular skill set and specialise in a certain area, in the same way that a solicitor will specialise in family law, commercial litigation or some other legal discipline. My affinity over the years has been process definition and Financial Control. I have always leaned in this direction, even in my more junior roles, where I had slightly less influence but was still able to effect change.

In my later career as a Finance Director, this speciality was often the specific reason for my appointment and I developed a track record for 'fixing' businesses which were struggling with their finances and, as a result, their strategy. Establishing control not only improved the liquid finances of the business but also provided a solid platform from which profitable growth became almost inevitable. As these businesses grew, the financial controls also scaled, enabling the directors to evolve their strategy around the performance of the organisation.

I have written this book as a result of my experiences over the years, as well as my desire to make businesses more secure. The main reason for this, if I'm completely honest, is because I have seen too many businesses fail due to poor Financial Control and the aftermath is not pretty, in fact it has had a profound impact on me as a person. During the course of my career, I have had to carry out some awful duties, such as calling a single mother on maternity leave to inform her that the company had ceased trading and there would be no job for her to return to. Telling a small supplier that they wouldn't be getting paid, as our business had collapsed, knowing that this would also be the end of their business. I have plenty of similar examples and, in all cases, establishing financial controls would have saved the day, or at least allowed the business to come to a more natural end, without impacting so many innocent parties.

I will admit that my career has given me something of a bias. I am more cynical and forensic in my approach than most and I often want to see something with my own eyes, check a formula or review a reconciliation before I will accept that things are the way they seem. I can also quickly recognise the signs of stress in a struggling FD and I have established a framework to pick up a 'dropped ball' even when the person who dropped it is no longer around.

My experiences are not typical, but they're not as rare as you might think either.

Of course, most SMEs (which make up the majority of my audience) don't have a Finance Director, they use an external accountant, or firm of accountants. In many ways this is worse, as the owner of the business is happy that they have delegated control and takes their eye off the ball completely. This book will explain why this is a bad, sometimes catastrophic, move and give you the knowledge to counteract it.

My Purpose and Passion

So why did I write this book? It's not because I want businesses to have more control over their finances. Of course I do want that, but it's more of a side-effect. What I really want is directors, owners and senior managers of businesses to understand how finance *really* works. Who is accountable for what. What the numbers actually mean. How to engineer the growth you want for your business and how to improve your profitability by making the right decisions.

A big part of this is giving MDs enough Finance knowledge to be able to challenge their FD or external accountant, so that they understand where the accountability lies. Having worked for and with many SMEs as both an FD and a consultant, I know that the vast majority of owners/MDs do not know enough about finance to confidently challenge their accountant/FD or reliably make the right decisions for their business. I have explained financial concepts to MDs, only for them to look blankly at me and tell me they 'don't need to know this stuff'. I disagree.

The Conditions of Control outlined in Chapter 5 of this book place the accountability firmly with the MD for the facilitation of control in their own business. Without these conditions, the likelihood that a: you will achieve control and b: you will maintain that control as the business grows, is minimal. That's why the concepts are outlined first, so that you can truly understand how big a piece of work this is, but how powerful it can become as your business grows.

This is why an MD needs to know all this 'finance stuff'. Many MDs I have worked with have told me they don't need to know what I'm trying to explain to them, as long as I know it. I don't agree with that sentiment because although I do know it, you're ultimately accountable for it, so you need to know it too. Not only that, but you need to know that I know it. If the MD can't hold the FD (or accountant) accountable then no one will be able to. If you don't understand finance well enough to challenge the person you have delegated it to, you can't possibly be accountable for it.

It's also crucial that challenges are presented in the right way and that the MD creates a culture and environment where the FD or accountant expects to be challenged and doesn't fear it. I've seen people laughed at, shouted at, humiliated, degraded and even dismissed for making mistakes. I have also seen people break down in tears because something is wrong and there's no time to fix it. They're so terrified of the reaction that they 'fix it' the easy way, by changing an Excel formula or fudging a number. The idea that people become infallible beyond a certain level is fundamentally flawed and a high salary is no substitute for a healthy, supportive culture. I have worked in many different environments over the years and an oppressive, blame-oriented culture is not conducive to success in any business or industry.

Remember, the MD of a business may not be responsible for all of the day-to-day activities but they are accountable for everything. This book is based on that principle, so if you don't agree with this concept, you may not agree with much else I say. Give me a chance and read it anyway. Hopefully I can change your mind.

Chapter 2 - What is Financial Control?

NB: I often skip forewords or introductions to books, usually because I assume they will just be self-aggrandising anecdotes or thanking the author's wife or lecturer or dog. I may be wrong and I might have missed some priceless pearls of wisdom, but it's too late now to go back and find out. The introduction to this book contains no thanks and no anecdotes, but it does provide the context required to get the most out of this book. Without it, you will probably spend the rest of the book shaking your head and muttering about how I don't know what I'm talking about or something. Please go back and read it if you haven't already. It's less than 3,000 words and you can read that in no time. Thanks

Why Do I Need Financial Control in my Business?

If you have a product or service which is very marketable, extremely valuable to a wide range of customers, brings in a healthy profit margin and cannot be replicated by anyone else, will never be superseded or made obsolete by technological advances and is impervious to changes in customer needs, then you don't really need to worry about financial controls. You'll probably be fine.

I mean, you should still implement these controls, and your business will be even more profitable if you do, but the implausibly favourable conditions listed above will probably be enough for your business to thrive.

For everyone else (99.9% of businesses), you will need to track your profit margins, control your costs, analyse your sales, guard against external threats, maximise opportunities, employ your resources effectively and ultimately grow your business and your profits to safeguard your future. In order to do this, you need to understand every aspect of your business, make timely decisions and have confidence that they are the correct decisions. The only way to do that is to establish control over your business and generate accurate and meaningful data. Our Four Points of Control framework will enable you to do this.

So what is the definition of 'Financial Control'? I mean the concept, rather than the phrase, since I would assume that most people reading this book can decipher what those two words mean.

The Elements of Control

Financial Control, in the context of our framework, comes down to three elements:

1. Performance Evaluation
2. Economic Viability
3. Compliance

These three elements cover every aspect of control in business. They also expose the reasons for failure. The vast majority (if not all) of businesses that fail (by which I mean cease trading permanently) will do so because they disregarded (or were not aware of) one or more of these elements. In many cases it will be all three, since they are (as you will see later in the book) interconnected and support each other. Maintaining them is a matter of discipline, so it stands to reason that if one of them is neglected, they will all be neglected, either through ignorance or an inherent lack of discipline.

The elements can be re-framed into a more practical format by looking at the questions each one ponders.

Performance Evaluation = "How are we doing?"
Economic Viability = "Is it good enough and if so, is it sustainable?"
Compliance = "Are we doing it the right way?"

The end goal, when you know you have established control, is to provide answers to these questions.
But of course the answers need to be quantified. Technically, you could answer these questions right now:

How are we doing? - "Pretty good I reckon"
Is it good enough? - "Well I think so"
Is it sustainable? - "Yeah, I think we'll be fine"
Are we doing it the right way? - "Yep"

There you go, you've answered the questions. Job done.

Of course these are not really answers. They are opinions. The real challenge is to relate your answers to an objective standard. To make sure all the answers are backed up by evidence and, above all, to keep reviewing your answers and checking your evidence consistently over time.

The answers below are not based on opinion or conjecture, they are based on **current data.** Data can change, but if you adhere to the principles outlined in this book and build the culture and infrastructure to support those principles, you will be able to establish the three elements of control to some degree. Once they've been established, it's just a case of tightening your control by reviewing the data and maintaining your processes.

How are we doing? - "The data shows that we are currently doing x% better than we expected to, and what we expected to do was sufficient to ensure survival of the business."

Is it good enough? - "Yes, the data shows that there is a significant margin between our actual results and what we need to do in order to survive, so results so far are at least good enough"

Is it sustainable? - "Market and supply chain factors we are aware of, and can reliably measure, suggest that we will have no problem maintaining our current trajectory. There are external events on the horizon but we have analysed them in terms of the risk they pose currently, and will update that analysis regularly, so there is no reason to think the business is not sustainable at this point."

Are we doing it the right way? - "All our external obligations have been met and we are on course to meet our voluntary commitments too."

By the time you reach the end of this book, you will know how to answer these questions with objective evidence. You will also understand how to continually review your data, make changes to your processes and ensure that the answers given are always the 'right' ones, because they will be the only answers you can arrive at using the data available.

Why SMEs?

The Four Points of Control framework is applicable to all businesses, regardless of size, industry or sector, since it focuses on fundamental elements which apply to all businesses, even those without the pressure of shareholders or profit expectations.

However, this book is primarily aimed at the owners or leaders of SME or startup businesses. The reason for this is that although many 'blue chip' businesses still have significant control deficiencies and may not even be aware of those deficiencies, they are generally large enough and profitable enough to weather the storm. To become a large business in the first place, they must have achieved a level of control and/or profitability to overcome their challenges, otherwise they would no longer exist.

It's worth noting, however, that even commercial behemoths fail from time to time. Businesses who are seemingly bulletproof can still falter and collapse. The difference is that, in many cases, they are too big to simply fade from existence completely. They are often acquired by a competitor or assimilated into a larger group of companies, often continuing under the same name, but with different operators.

Even at this level, if you care enough to take a look at the facts around their demise, you will find the same root causes of failure. Neglecting the three elements of control: Performance Evaluation, Economic Viability and Compliance, will still be at the heart of the collapse. In many cases, the size of the business works against them, since they are no longer agile or responsive enough to make swift, meaningful changes.

Many large companies don't take the time in their early years to instil the control processes outlined in this book and then find themselves struggling to understand why they no longer have the profitability, market share, turnover or competitive advantage they once enjoyed. Applying the Four Points of Control framework at that stage can be done, but it takes time, and time is a precious commodity, especially once the wheels start to fall off.

By contrast, smaller companies can adopt and change processes considerably more easily. They can make changes to their culture and build an infrastructure in a short space of time with minimal effort. They can design and implement a process in the same day, with one person making most of the key decisions. This means that they can try different things to see what works and then once they find something suitable, they can document it and build on it. It will then scale up as the business grows and ensure that control is maintained, not just in the early years but decades later.

On the other hand, smaller companies are also prone to knee-jerk decision making and erratic strategies. One person making the key decisions can be a double-edged sword if the person making the decisions doesn't take the time to facilitate control and work on the environment before trying to establish control.

The reason this book is focused on SMEs and startups is because the earlier you implement financial control, the greater your chances of survival and the more familiar you will become with the concepts and processes outlined in this book. The more familiar you are, the more intrinsic and automatic the elements of control will become in your business.

In the next chapter, you will learn the importance of the second and third year in business. Those who survive their first year have certainly earned a pat on the back, but the work is only just beginning and getting these processes in place as early as possible is vital to ensure your progression.

Chapter 3 - Why do we Need Financial Control?

The Benefits of Establishing Financial Control in your Business

When I was working as a Finance Director, no one asked why I was preoccupied with Financial Control. It was literally my job. As a consultant, however, I have often heard the comment below (or a variation of it) from my clients when I first meet them:

"I'm not bothered about Financial Control, I want to improve profitability/cut costs/grow my business."

To say they're amazed when I link these concepts together would probably be an overstatement, but when I explain that establishing Financial Control leads to total control of your business, allowing you to direct it in any way you like, maximising margins, reducing costs and achieving profitable growth, I often see a lightbulb switching on in their brain.

Working through the Four Points of Control framework will first establish stability in a business, ensuring economic survival. Maintaining the framework beyond that point makes it inevitable that stability turns to growth. Not the growth many businesses aim for (turnover) but the more meaningful and tangible growth of profit. Because the framework targets all elements of the business, it will flush out inefficiencies and cost-saving opportunities as well as margin improvements.

An increase in sales is still subject to a margin before it drops to the bottom line. A reduction in cost or an improvement in operational efficiency is usually 100% profit unless it also has a detrimental effect on sales. This is why the framework pushes from both ends and, if followed comprehensively, leads to improvements in all areas.

This is undoubtedly the biggest benefit to the pursuit of Financial Control and you will see in later chapters how this works in practise. However, there are also organic benefits which occur naturally during the process of establishing control, such as:

- Deeper understanding of the financial elements of business
- Fewer problems around compliance/regulation
- Heightened awareness of the reasons behind failure **and** success
- Improved data integrity
- Better decision making
- An infrastructure for the future
- Cultural improvements

The 20/60 Rule

All of the benefits mentioned so far are actually side-effects and not the express purpose of the Four Points of Control framework. The true purpose is far simpler. Survival.

That may seem dramatic, but the statistical likelihood of a new business in the UK surviving beyond the first three years is actually relatively low. The concept of 'the 20/60 rule' is that 20% of businesses fail in the first year, whereas 60% fail before the end of year three.

It doesn't take a maths whiz to realise then that 80% of businesses are statistically likely to survive year one, whereas only 40% will survive to the end of year three. These statistics are fairly stable and although there are undoubtedly fluctuations in individual years (for example, the COVID-19 pandemic caused a significant skewing of these percentages), the overall ratio has been consistent for decades and applies to many western countries, not just the UK.

Even if the specific statistics change over time and the ratio fluctuates, the principle remains the same. Most business will survive the first year, for several reasons, but those reasons will begin to exhaust themselves from year two onwards.

In year one, there are multiple factors which combine to support a business and boost motivation, such as:

1. Support from friends and family
2. Clear vision of what you want to achieve
3. Delusional view of how the business is doing
4. Government support initiatives for new businesses
5. Initial capital reserves
6. Promotional resources (many of these are discounted/free in year one)
7. Minimal overheads
8. Minimal obligations
9. Sky-high motivation and enthusiasm

This list is far from exhaustive, but you get the point. I'm not saying it's easy to start and run a business for one year, but it's statistically easier in year one than in subsequent years.

These elements are part of the reason a business may begin to falter in the second and third years, but the root of the 20/60 rule is simple. Point 3 in the above list - 'Delusional view of how the business is doing'. This is also the one you can actually do something about.

Reporting Regulations

In the UK, when a business completes its financial year (ie the twelve-month trading period, which may differ from the calendar year), the directors of a business must compile and approve the financial statements (or 'accounts') relating to that year. Once approved, these statements are filed with a government agency known as Companies House and, once filed, become a matter of public record, which anyone can view. This process is generally known as 'filing the accounts' of the business.

The business has a nine-month period after the end of its financial year to file the accounts with Companies House. This is to allow the company sufficient time to prepare, reconcile, amend, review and finally approve the financial statements, confirming that they represent a true and fair view of the financial position of the company. Some companies are of such size and complexity that nine months is scarcely enough. These companies often require an audit from an external firm of accountants to verify that the numbers are consistent with the company's own accounting policies and applicable financial reporting standards. This audit in itself can take several months to complete.

However, many companies don't need anywhere near nine months to finalise and approve their financial statements. Small companies with simple operations, few employees and minimal stakeholders should be able to complete their financial statements within a couple of months at most.

The problem with allowing this amount of time is that most companies will take advantage of it and not even think about filing their accounts until the deadline is looming. This may not seem like a problem but ultimately it's the root of the 20/60 rule. This delayed completion of the year-end reporting means that many companies have no idea how well, or how badly, their business is performing until nine months after the end of their first year, which, of course, is **twenty one months** after they started trading.

Apart from the delayed reporting timescale, small and medium-sized companies are held to different reporting standards depending on their size. The majority of companies in the UK are not required to submit profit and loss reports with their financial statements and are exempt from audit. This means that until the ninth month of year two, they are not required to produce any reporting whatsoever, or engage any external party to review what they've been doing. This can be disastrous for their business, since the approach many businesses take is one or both of the following:

- Our accountant has it covered, let's just concentrate on running the business.
- Nine months? That's ages away, let's cross that bridge when we come to it.

In reality, in my experience at least, all businesses know two things at the end of year one: Turnover and cash balance. Anything else they claim to know is flawed unless they have been producing reliable monthly reporting and, in many instances, they're pretty shocked when they receive their year end figures from their accountant.

The 20/60 Rule in Effect

Below is a typical timeline of how the 20/60 Rule manifests itself. I have seen this happen many times and the approach and thought processes are broadly similar, even if the specific actions are different.

1st January 20X1 - Business is launched

31st December 20X1 - Year one draws to a close. Sales have been strong and we have cash in the bank. Not sure about profit but it must be decent, as we've survived year one and have cash in the bank. High fives all round

1st January 20X2 - Year two begins, this time next year we'll be millionaires.

31st March 20X2 - End of the first quarter of year two. Cash is running low. Not sure what's happened, especially since our first year was so successful. Decided to spend more on marketing to drive sales.

30th June 20X2 - End of quarter two. Managed to get a loan from the bank. Not much, as they wanted to see draft accounts for year one and we don't have them yet, but it's enough to help with our cash flow problems and get us back on track.

30th September 20X2 - The accountant has filed the accounts for year one. They can't be right as it shows we made a loss, but we had money in the bank in December so I don't know what he's done. Not happy. Apparently the dividends I took in year one have now had to be reclassified as director's loans because there wasn't enough profit or something. Now I owe the business money. I don't get it.

31st December 20X2 - End of year two. I'm exhausted. I've worked like a dog all year and there's no money in the bank. Might have to remortgage the house.

1st January 20X3 - Here we go again. Just need to get sales up and we'll be fine. It's all about turnover.

31st March 20X3 - Managed to borrow some more money, paid a new marketing company to get turnover up. Right decision I think.

30th June 20X3 - Marketing spend seems to be working. Sales are back up to where they were in year one. Although we still don't have a lot of money in the bank and now we have loan repayments to make. I don't understand it.

30th September 20X3 - Just got the accounts for year two. They're WORSE than year one and the balance sheet is negative because of the borrowings. I don't know what to do.

31st December 20X3 - New job starts on 5th January. Actually looking forward to it. Starting my own business was the biggest mistake I ever made.

The fundamental problem is a lack of accountability, a lack of understanding and, most of all, a lack of data. I have seen many business owners over the years receive their accounts for their first year's trading and express confusion and panic. The results do not correlate with their innate 'feeling' of how the business has performed.

Imagine if you wanted to lose weight and started a new diet. You weigh in on day one and record your weight. Then you don't step on the scales until twenty one months later. In the intervening period you just rely on how you look in the mirror and whether you 'feel' heavier or lighter. Then when you do eventually weigh yourself, you stare incredulously at the number on the scales and mutter "That can't be right".

Ok, that's a facetious analogy, but the principle stands. If you don't measure the performance of your business from day one until day SIX HUNDRED AND THIRTY SEVEN, when the government forces you to do it, that's a pretty serious dereliction of duty, especially if you have employees and creditors relying on you.

To properly manage a business, you need to analyse and evaluate the performance of that business. You need to assess whether or not the business is economically viable and you need to determine whether or not the business is compliant in its external obligations. You can't wait until a government agency forces you to ascertain this information. You need to do it yourself, well before you are required to. This isn't the only way to run a successful business, but it's the only way to ensure that a business is as successful as it could be. To do any less is to take unnecessary risks.

The reality is that the vast majority of SMEs could prepare and finalise their accounts very quickly and make data-led decisions in time to implement them in the new financial year, but because they don't have to, they choose not to. They could also implement a reporting framework to ensure financial control during the year, but again they often choose not to.

One of the reasons for this is that they have essentially abdicated their responsibility for finance as soon as they appointed their accountant. I can understand this to some extent. After all they didn't start a business to manage Finance, Health and Safety or Human Resources. They started a business to do what they always dreamed of, or at least something they have an interest in. Not Finance - bleurgh.

Many of the MDs I have worked with have no interest in Finance at all. They don't like it. They don't really understand it and they don't actually think they need to understand it. Many of them think that appointing an accountant absolves them of their responsibility in this area. They are incorrect.

Accountants - What do they ACTUALLY do?

One of the reasons many business owners do not rush to file their accounts and don't introduce financial controls is because they have appointed an accountant. This gives them the illusion that everything is under control and the accountability has been delegated. In many cases, it has actually been abdicated.

Unfortunately, it's a common misconception among SME owners that, once you've appointed an accountant, you no longer need to worry about your finances. This is not the case. Even if your business grows to the point where an annual audit becomes a legal requirement, the accountability for the accuracy of the finances remains with the directors of the business. It's important that you don't lose sight of this.

Many of the SME clients I have worked with have fundamentally misunderstood what accountants do and (to a lesser extent) where the accountability sits when it comes to the accounts of the business.

"I get a great deal from my accountant"

Countless times, I have heard "I get a great deal from my accountant" from my clients when I first meet them. This is usually followed (later in the same conversation) by "Oh my accountant doesn't do that" and shortly after "Why isn't my accountant doing that/telling me this?".

What they generally mean is that they don't pay their accountant a lot of money. This is not a 'great deal', it's a cheap deal, and, as is often the case, you get what you pay for.

The problem here is that many business owners view accountants in the same way most of us view car insurance. It's a legal requirement and we have to pay for it, so let's get it as cheap as possible. This is based on the incorrect belief that you need an accountant if you're in business. This is not the case at all. In fact, until you reach the threshold at which you are no longer considered a micro or small business, there is no requirement for audit and an accountant is not mandatory.

Ultimately, your accountant is there to help. The nature of this help is around the accounting treatment of transactions and the calculation of tax liabilities. Nowadays, they will often do this for a relatively inexpensive fee, because the advent of cloud-based accounting software has put certain elements of finance in the hands of the business owner or their staff.

This technological evolution has led to an unprecedented set of circumstances. The old stereotype of a business owner dropping off a box of invoices to their accountant at the end of the year, and then the accountant creating a set of accounts, is a far cry from today. Nowadays, a business can manage their own book-keeping during the year, posting their own payroll journals and managing their own VAT etc. Then, at the end of the year, they can just tell their accountant that the software has been updated and the accountant can log in, download the required data and then file the accounts.

The problem with this approach is that neither party is necessarily in a position to accurately verify the financial position of the business, which is what the annual accounts are supposed to achieve. Rather than the business owner running the business and the accountant preparing the accounts, as in the 'olden days', we now have a situation where the business does a half-arsed job of managing their finances and then assumes that the accountant will sort it all out at year end. The reason this dysfunctional arrangement has materialised is that the business owner has access to the systems to manage their accounts, but they don't have the accounting knowledge to do it properly. Similarly, the accountant no longer has the data and documentation to create a full year's accounts and is reliant on the business to present them with an accurate set of data at the end of the year.

Another development in recent years, which compounds this issue, is that the use of cloud-based accounting software has led to the overall service provided by accountants morphing into something quite different. This in turn has led to a comparative reduction in fees and the market has become extremely competitive. Accountants will often charge £100-£150 per month for a service that would previously have cost far more.

This is the perfect storm that leads to my clients telling me they get a 'great deal' from their accountant. It's not a great deal. When you consider what a qualified accountant can earn, £150 is buying you a small amount of attention on a monthly basis. You will not get in-depth monthly reporting for this fee. Nor will you get support with the creation of a budget (arguably the most important part of your financial controls). You won't get analysis or comprehensive advice. You will get year-end accounts and calculation of your tax liabilities. That's it.

So let's bust a few myths when it comes to accountants.

'Accounting' essentially means to account for transactions. The etymology of this verb includes words such as 'reckon' and 'count'. In real terms it means to ensure that a transaction has been accounted for, or **treated** correctly. You may hear the term 'accounting treatment' on occasion. This translates as, 'has this transaction been reflected in the right place and time'. The place is an account in your accounting system and the time is the period in which it should be recognised.

Data analysis, general business advice, book-keeping, strategic planning, credit control, budgeting, forecasting, cash management and reporting are all services an accountant can provide, but they do not usually form part of the standard package of services most accountants offer. Your accountant is probably not doing these things for you unless you have specifically asked them to (and are paying them to).

This isn't a criticism of accountants, by the way. That 'great deal' you're getting from your accountant is precisely because they don't have to prepare a full set of accounts from scratch, which means they can charge you less because they are doing less, and that's my point. Many business owners think that if they have an accountant on board, then ALL of their financial concerns are now covered and they can essentially forget about Finance and get on with making their millions. In reality there are significant gaps between what your accountant does and what your business needs to ensure survival and prosperity. If you don't want to bridge that gap, then you'd better be paying someone else to, or your business will soon be out of control and you won't be able to blame your accountant.

'Signing off'

Another myth I often have to address with my clients is the concept that an accountant 'signs off' the accounts of the business. I have met countless business owners who have used the phrase 'sign off' in this context, as if their accountant has taken accountability for the accounts and will be liable if anything is found to be incorrect. This is not the case. The Companies Act (2006) does indeed state that the annual accounts should be approved and signed - by a director of the company. Not an accountant.

Ultimately, the Financial Statements of the business are the responsibility of the directors, and that's where the accountability remains. Of course, the accountant is responsible for any advice they may have given, or errors in the tax computations or any other calculations they have carried out, but not for errors made by you or your book-keeper during the year. Once you have approved the accounts, the accountability and responsibility for them is yours.

Breaking the 20/60 Rule

Two traits often found in failed (or failing) business owners are:

1. Not knowing what they **should** know
2. Not knowing what they **don't** know

The vast majority of business owners know their product or service very well. Those who go on to be successful are those who dedicate some time to learning the things they **don't** know, so that they can cover all the bases.

Ultimately, the reason we need to establish Financial Control is to 'break' the 20/60 Rule. We will explore this in more detail in the next chapter and ensure that your business is one of the 40% that survives beyond year three.

Chapter 4 - Breaking the '20/60 Rule'

How To Break the 20/60 Rule

So how do we break the 20/60 rule and ensure the stability (and ultimately the profitable growth) of a business? As with many things, it's simple, but it's not easy.

As mentioned already in this book, the key to breaking the 20/60 Rule and ensuring the longevity of your business is to establish and maintain the three elements of control:

- Performance Evaluation
- Economic Viability
- Compliance

The key to achieving all three of these elements, and therefore the ultimate goal, is **the correct calculation of profit.** That's it. That's what everything in this book boils down to.

So why is this so vital? The simple fact is that without correctly calculating the profit your business is currently making, and is capable of making in the future, you can't possibly begin to evaluate your performance, or assess your economic viability, or ensure your compliance.

It's vital to recognise that to achieve control of your business, these elements must first be established and then consistently maintained. Establishing them from scratch, especially if the business has been trading for some time, can be very hard work, and that work is all in vain if they are not maintained.

The most efficient way to maintain the elements of control is to use The Control Cycle.

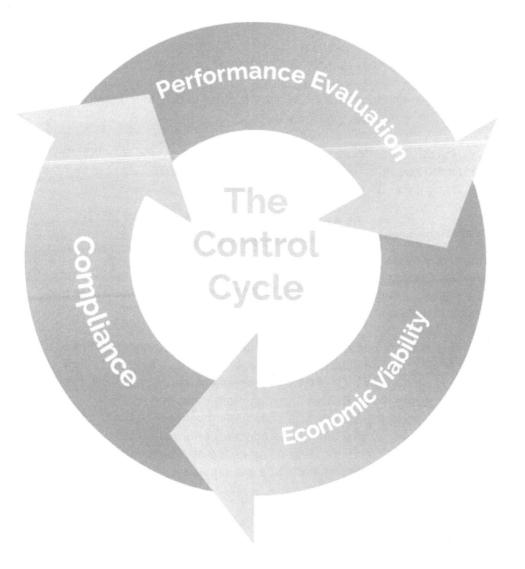

The Control Cycle is a mechanism by which the three elements are measured and analysed on a periodic basis, ideally monthly. It's important to accept that it's unlikely that you will ever achieve 100% control of your business, and even if you do, it will be fleeting. The reporting parameters and competitive advantages in business can change overnight and inefficiencies can appear from nowhere, even if you have your 'finger on the pulse' of your business or industry.

We'll revisit the Control Cycle in a later chapter but let's look at the elements of control individually.

Performance Evaluation

Performance Evaluation, simply put, means "How are we doing?"

Not "How have we done?" or "How are we going to do?" but "How are we doing?"

This might seem like I'm splitting hairs, but what I mean is that the performance needs to be gauged **against** something. You don't know how you're doing if you don't how you **should** be doing.

The subtle difference between "How have we done?" and "How are we doing?" also marks the difference between year-end accounts and in-year performance evaluation. Year-end accounts give you the results when it's too late to do anything to change them. Monthly performance evaluation enables you to make meaningful changes during the year, empowering you to take control and influence your own results.

This is a vital part of running a business. But what if you don't know how to objectively measure your performance, or don't have time to do it, or just don't really want to do it. Or maybe you already measure your performance but you're getting it wrong. This happens more often that you may think and without understanding the three key accounting concepts we will look at later in this book, you may well be measuring your performance incorrectly. It may be immaterial at the moment, depending on the size of your business, but as your business grows, getting the right tools in place is essential, so that they can scale up with the business.

There are many tools available for measuring the performance of a business. Sales reports, stock usage reports, labour efficiency, KPI reporting, score cards and others. These all play an important role in the day-to-day management of a business. But they are not foolproof.

Ultimately, the reason financial control, if established properly, results in total control of a business, is down to two factors:

- **Accounting concepts** - You need to calculate your profit using the same methods your accountant will use at the end of the year, otherwise you will have a surprise at year end.
- **Comparative reporting** - You need to benchmark your performance against comparatives in order to understand your progress.

These two factors combine to create flawlessly reliable data, which is presented in the form of Management Accounts. You may already produce Management Accounts in your business, but unless you have incorporated the characteristics referred to above, your Management Accounts are not sufficient to provide the levels of performance evaluation required to establish control.

If this is the case, you are far from alone. I have seen all manner of 'Management Accounts', which are actually not Management Accounts at all.

Management Accounts should comprise **at least** the following statements:

- Profit & Loss/Income Statement
- Balance Sheet/Statement of Financial Position
- Cash Flow Statement

They often include other supporting reports, but if they don't include these three statements as a minimum, they are not Management Accounts.

Similarly, if they don't include comparative reporting and are not compiled in accordance with accounting concepts, they are not Management Accounts.

These elements are explained in more detail in Chapter 6, so I won't get too detailed at this point.

Economic Viability

As I'm sure you already know, a business needs to be economically viable in order to survive. In the context of this book, Economic Viability is fairly simple. Once Performance Evaluation has been carried out (ie Management Accounts have been created), we know 'how we're doing'. Next, we need to answer the following questions:

- Is it good enough?
- Is it sustainable?

In other words:

- Can we survive in the **current** economic environment?
- Will we flourish in the **future** economic environment?

This is always tough, as the answer could simply be "No".

If your performance evaluation shows that you're losing money, and there is no way to reverse this, then the business is, in all likelihood, not a viable enterprise. This may be a bitter pill to swallow, but hopefully you've discovered it in time to either cut your losses and get out, or to seek help. Either way, it's better to know now and wind things up voluntarily than to continue blindly losing money until you're forced to call it a day.

But for our purposes, we'll assume that this isn't the case and the performance evaluation shows that the business is at least viable in the current economic environment. This is established through your comparative reporting, using breakeven analysis. Put simply, if you achieve at least your breakeven turnover, your business will survive. Of course, you first need to ascertain your breakeven turnover, but we'll get to that later.

The next question is whether you can survive in the future economic environment. This is much harder to determine, as you would need to not only estimate your future breakeven turnover, which would require advance knowledge of your costs and profit margins, but you would also need to predict the conditions of the environment in which your future business operates. This sounds like a tough task, but fear not - we have techniques in Chapter 15 that will help with this.

Compliance

Compliance is otherwise expressed as "Are we doing the right thing?" or to put it in more specific terms "Are we meeting our external obligations".

It's vital to meet your corporate obligations, otherwise you could work on your Performance Evaluation and determine that your business is viable and sustainable, but then come unstuck as a result of an unforeseen external problem. An obvious example of this would probably be government agencies such as HMRC or Companies House, but there are many others.

For example, consider an e-commerce seller who makes most of their sales on Amazon. Amazon imposes conditions on their sellers, often centred around delivery times, returns and other customer service factors. Having spent decades building trust and loyalty with online shoppers, they are not about to let their sellers undermine their efforts. If you want to sell on their platform, you need to abide by their rules. If you fail to do this, they can impose sanctions on your account, withhold disbursements, restrict your selling ability or even ban you completely. In some cases funds can be withheld for months while the seller tries desperately to get their seller rating up to satisfactory levels. In some cases this can be enough to put an already-struggling business out of action permanently.

Compliance doesn't just mean mandatory obligations either. Corporate and Social Responsibilities may include voluntary initiatives, which produce lucrative PR benefits, especially in the age of social media. However, saying you're going to do something and then failing to do it can reverse this effect and have a catastrophic effect on the public image of a business.

The End Goal

"Begin with the end in mind" - Stephen R Covey

This chapter outlines the three elements of control we are striving to achieve. It's important to keep them in mind as you progress through this book and as you run your business. These elements of control are the end goal and if you can master the techniques and processes that lead to this goal, your business **will** be successful.

Achieving and maintaining the three elements of control will mean that you have established control to the extent that it's possible to establish control. Getting there is a three-part process:

1. Facilitate control
2. Establish control
3. Maintain control

We'll look at facilitating control in the next chapter.

Chapter 5 - Facilitating Control

The Conditions of Control

In order to facilitate control, you need to prepare the environment and culture around you to give your efforts towards establishing control the best chance of success.

I could use an analogy about planting a seed and preparing the ground so that the seed has the best chance of growing. To be honest, I don't know much about gardening, so there's no point making that analogy, as I would probably get it wrong. I don't think an analogy is really necessary anyway, as this is pretty straightforward.

If the MD/CEO doesn't accept their accountability for the financial controls of the business, and the person they delegate that accountability to is unable to accept it (by virtue of the fact that they don't have ultimate control of the business) then no one will be accountable. When something falls through the cracks, the parties will blame each other and the actual cause will be unknown and irrelevant, because neither party will take it upon themselves to fix the problem. In this scenario, it's the business that.

If the MD doesn't understand finance well enough to challenge their accountant or Finance Director, then how can they understand or accept their accountability. If they ask their accountant/FD a question and don't understand the answer, then how can they possibly make the decisions necessary to drive the business forward.

If you have a culture where people are afraid to tell you the truth and therefore lie to you in order to avoid your wrath, then holding them to account is largely pointless. You won't get straight answers, you'll just get good news, and the value of bad news will be lost.

The scenarios described above show the conditions of control (or the lack of them) in a nutshell. To be able to establish control, you first need to create an environment based on the following three conditions:

Acceptance of accountability

Challenge through understanding

No-fear environment

These conditions can only be driven and encouraged from the top. It all starts with the MD. He or she must lead by example, build the infrastructure and create conditions which lead to a culture conducive to fostering a controlled environment which will benefit everyone.

Condition 1: Acceptance of Accountability - The 'Braking Distance' Principle

When driving, in the UK at least, if you collide with the rear end of another car, there are very few scenarios in which the police (and the insurance company) will place the blame anywhere other than at your door. The reason for this is that you are expected to leave enough distance between your car and the vehicle ahead in order to stop safely, no matter what the conditions are. If the road is wet - your fault. If the guy in front braked suddenly - your fault. If visibility is poor due to fog - your fault.

In all of these cases, if you leave enough time and distance to react, there would be no accident. This principle applies to business too, and the Braking Distance Principle is a key theory we will keep referring to throughout the book.

As the owner, MD or leader of a business, you are accountable for everything, including the finances. I know most business owners will agree with this statement. They always do when directly asked, but their behaviour sometimes undermines their words. I have spoken with clients who readily agree that they are accountable for everything, but then explain how they leave all their 'financial stuff' to their accountant.

The majority of business owners I have worked with at SME level are passionate about the product or service their business supplies. In many cases it was their passion before they launched their business. They may have studied it at university, or grown up around it (in the case of family businesses). Because of this, they will maintain an active interest in the production and sales side of the business, even if they eventually delegate the responsibility for managing these elements to others. Even then, they will make their sales staff and operations managers' lives a misery by constantly showing up in their offices to 'check in' (or interfere). This is natural and understandable, given their passion for the product.

The same level of interest often doesn't exist for the supporting functions of the business, such as HR, Health and Safety and Finance. The preferred approach to these elements is often 'someone else can sort that out'.

However, the accountability for all of these elements remains with the MD, no matter who the responsibility is delegated to and no matter which bits the MD would prefer to be involved in. The important point to remember is that responsibility can be delegated or shared, accountability is always retained.

Even if an FD is appointed, and even if they are paid more than anyone else in the company, even if he or she is vastly qualified and experienced, the MD will always be accountable for the finances of the business. The same applies if an external accountant is appointed.

The first step towards facilitating control and the first condition of control is complete acceptance by the MD that he or she is ultimately accountable for the financial controls of the business, even if there is a fully qualified and highly experienced Finance Director or accountant in place. Delegation should not become abdication.

Condition 2: Challenge Through Understanding - Arm Yourself with Knowledge

If the first condition is fulfilled and the MD accepts that he or she is accountable for the financial controls of the business, condition two would appear to be pretty obvious. After all, how can you be accountable for a subject you don't understand? Nevertheless, my experience is that the majority of SME owners and MDs are not knowledgeable enough about Finance to truly accept their accountability, or even hold their financial support staff accountable.

In order to thoroughly understand and analyse financial statements, and therefore make the right decisions in directing your business, you need to be able to ask the right questions and, crucially, understand the answers you're given. Even to recruit your finance team, you need to know what questions to ask at interview and what the answers mean. I have heard countless business owners and MDs over the years defer to their accountant on any financial question.

There are three accounting concepts I believe all business owners and directors need to understand and be familiar with. Many of them are, but the majority are not, as I have learned from experience. As with many of the concepts dealt with in this book, the divide seems to be between SMEs and Blue Chips. To be a director at a large company, an understanding of accounting concepts is generally assumed. However, there is no requirement to learn such things before you start your own business. In fact, the misconception I have often found is that as long as you get an accountant on board in the early days, you don't need to know anything at all about finance. This is incorrect, and many business owners are surprised when I tell them there is no requirement to have an accountant at all until your business reaches a certain level. Learning fundamental accounting concepts (which you would need to learn even if you did appoint an accountant, if you want to understand what they present to you) would, in many cases, enable you to file your own accounts, manage your own business finances and direct your business strategically and effectively.

The accounting concepts I refer to are detailed in Chapter 6. As with virtually all accounting concepts, they are logical and uncomplicated. Taking the time to understand them is not only vital in order to fully embrace the accountability that your statutory obligations as a director place on you, but crucial to creating stability and profitable growth in your business through establishing financial control.

Condition 3: No Fear Environment - Appreciate the Value of Bad News

Another key element required to become accountable is information. If you want honest information from people, you can't 'shoot the messenger'. You must learn to appreciate the value of bad news.

Many of life's changes and developments come from a negative place. You make a mistake, you learn from it. You do something wrong, you suffer and you learn not to do it again. It's no different in business. The difference is that when your business is small and you're doing everything yourself, you learn these lessons directly. As the business grows, you rely on others to tell you when something goes wrong.

Infrastructure

As with other terms in this book, the word 'Infrastructure' has different meanings in different contexts. We have a specific definition of this term in the context of the Four Points of Control. Ultimately, it breaks down to two key phrases:

"Who is responsible for what?"
"Who is accountable for what?"

Every significant aspect of your operation, including supporting functions, must have a designated responsible person, so that everyone in the business knows who to go to in the event of a problem, dispute or idea. Drawing up and publishing a register of responsibility, which shows everyone in the business the designated responsible person for any issue, is just as important as a list of company phone numbers.

This will improve efficiency in the business and minimise the likelihood of problems being allowed to fester. It can also form the basis of a training plan and lead to improvements in the overall culture of your business.

Culture

"If you want to build a ship, don't drum up people to collect wood and don't assign them tasks and work, but rather teach them to long for the endless immensity of the sea."

Antoine de Saint Exupéry
(French writer and aviator)

This quote sums it up for me. To really get your team on board, don't just give them instructions, instead create a yearning to succeed. Involving your team in the development and planning of your business, empowering them to make decisions and then holding them accountable for those decisions will ensure that you foster a collaborative and supportive culture which enhances the likelihood of your success.

A healthy and open culture is a vital part of facilitating control. Creating an environment in which people are comfortable with being challenged and forthcoming with 'negative' information is essential. The value of bad news should not be underestimated as every negative result is an opportunity for growth and improvement.

Negative outcomes are a major driver of positive change. Generally-speaking, more is learned from failure than from success and a culture in which mistakes are freely admitted (and lessons are learned) will progress more rapidly than an organisation where people are fearful of their boss's reaction.

Invest in Your Finance Setup

Many SMEs rely on an external accountant to manage their Finances. This is sometimes a mistake, as an external party won't have the intimate knowledge of your business necessary to generate meaningful data and advise on key decisions. Most of their advice will be based on their 'arms-length' understanding of your organisation, combined with theoretical guidance based on legislation and accounting standards, as opposed to commercial acumen.

A far better approach would be to employ someone in-house, who can get to know your business and understand all the key performance indicators impacting the finances on a periodic basis. They can support with compiling a budget and grow with your business.

Business owners will often invest heavily in their sales function but then scrimp on their finance setup but I   nvesting in good finance staff or paying more to your accountant to get some valuable strategic insight will pay off at least as much as enhancing your sales operation.

Ultimately, in order to establish control of your organisation, achieve profitable growth and safeguard the future of your business, the facilitation stage is vital. Building your infrastructure, fostering a positive culture and accepting your accountability is crucial to the development of your financial controls.

Chapter 6 - Essential Accounting Concepts

Why do I Need to Understand Accounting Concepts?

As you have no doubt noticed, I am a big fan of accountability in business. It's a major factor in the collapse of a business and many of the business failures I have seen were a direct result of the owners or directors delegating (or, more accurately, abdicating) their accountability and eventually pointing the finger at others. This is a flawed approach. Of course other people in the business may have caused the problem, whether through corruption, incompetence or error, but the person accountable for the business should have the knowledge and systems in place to ensure that they are aware of anything that could have such a devastating impact on their business.

Ultimately, if you run your business according to the 'Braking Distance' principle outlined earlier in this book, you will inevitably become more accountable, but part of this is arming yourself with knowledge and skills that will empower you to become truly accountable. That's why a sound understanding of accounting concepts is vital.

Remember the three conditions, which are vital to the facilitation of control.

Acceptance of accountability

Challenge through understanding

No-fear environment

This chapter focuses mainly on 'Challenge through understanding' as you will be unable to challenge your accountant or FD if you don't have the knowledge to do so.

To be clear, I'm not trying to turn you into an accountant. Business owners need to wear many hats and can't become too entrenched in any one area. But a sound understanding of these areas is vital to ensure that you ask the right questions, understand the answers and make the right decisions.

The other, arguably more important, reason you need to know these concepts is to ensure accuracy. Your accountant will prepare your statutory accounts in accordance with accounting standards, so your Management Accounts will need to follow suit, otherwise you will be ensuring surprises at year end. You will also see, later in the book, that these concepts are one of the main reasons Management Accounts are flawlessly reliable.

Ultimately, the accurate calculation of profit, in terms of both timing and numerical accuracy is vital. Without accurate profit calculations:

1. Your performance evaluation will be flawed - since profit is the end result.
2. You can't determine your economic viability - as profit is the main determining factor in viability.
3. You can't ensure compliance - because taxes and other liabilities are derived from profit.

In other words, all three elements of control will fail if profit is not calculated accurately and assigned to the correct period.

The Accounting Concepts you Need to Know

The good news is that there are only three accounting concepts you need to know and they are perfectly logical.

1. The Accounting Equation
2. Double Entry Accounting
3. The Accrual Accounting Convention

1. The Accounting Equation

The Accounting Equation is fairly simple:

Assets = (Liabilities + Equity)

Or to put it another way

Equity = (Assets - Liabilities)

'Equity' essentially means the combined capital of the business, which usually consists of share capital (the investment put in by the owner) and any profit or reserves retained by the business.

In a simple business, which the majority of SMEs are, Equity consists of share capital and profit. So for the purposes of this chapter, we will take 'equity' to mean 'retained profit'. **Retained** profit just means cumulative profit from all years the business has been trading.

So in this context, the Accounting Equation boils down to:

(Share Capital + Retained profit) = (Assets - Liabilities)

Share Capital in a non-listed limited company usually consists of a nominal value (eg £100), so for the purposes of the example below, we will ignore it and the only equity item will be profit.

The balance sheet of your business is where assets and liabilities are recorded. It's also where the equity (including profit) is shown. An example of a balance sheet is shown below:

Balance Sheet: January 2021	Jan-21
Fixed Assets	
Fixed assets - Office Equipment	3,582
Fixed assets - Plant & Machinery	14,856
Fixed assets - Motor Vehicles	9,855
Total Fixed Assts	28,293
Current Assets	
Accounts Receivable	27,856
Bank & cash Equivalents	42,887
Prepayments	5,246
Other current assets	452
Total Current Assets	76,441
Current Liabilities	
Accounts Payable	18,542
Accruals	11,244
PAYE Payable	2,585
VAT Liability	8,542
Pension contributions payable	845
Other current liabilities	642
Total Current Liabilities	42,400
Long Term Liabilities	
Loans	8,528
Hire purchase	1,419
Total Long Term Liabilities	9,947
NET ASSETS	52,387
Funded by:	
Share Capital	100
Current year profit	16,543
Retained Earnings	35,744
Dividends	0
EQUITY	52,387

The typical layout of a Balance Sheet is assets at the top, then liabilities, with equity shown at the bottom. In this example, we can see the following headings:

Total Fixed Assets	28,293
Total Current Assets	76,441
Total Current Liabilities	42,400
Total Long-Term Liabilities	9,947
Equity	52,387

From here, we should be able to calculate the Accounting Equation.

Total assets (28,293 + 76,441)	104,734
Total liabilities (42,400 + 9,947)	52,347
Total assets - Total liabilities	52,387
Equity	52,387

So you can see how the equation works. If you deduct the balance of your liabilities from the balance of your assets, this **must** be equivalent to your equity (capital + profit)

Assets & Liabilities

You may already know what assets and liabilities are, but here's a summary for those who don't:

The technical definition of an asset is "a resource with economic value that an individual, corporation, or country owns or controls with the expectation that it will provide a future benefit."

In simple terms, an asset is anything owned by the business, or owed to the business. Examples of common assets and how they fulfil the definition above are as follows:

Asset	Future economic benefit
Manufacturing machine	Processing of raw materials into products to be sold
Bank balance	Cash to be utilised for economic benefit
Raw material stock	Stock of material to be processed into finished goods and sold to customers
Finished goods stock	Stock of finished goods to be sold to customers
Company car	Used by sales staff in the process of generating sales revenue
Trade debtors	Payment of invoices to be received at a later date

A 'fixed asset' is an item over a certain value which is expected to remain in the business for   more than a year, and is not held for the purpose of resale. Examples of fixed assets in the list above would be the manufacturing machine and the company car.

Liabilities, conversely, are debts which the company owes and is obligated to pay in a future period. Liabilities are grouped into 'current' liabilities and 'long-term' liabilities. A current liability is generally considered to be any obligation which falls due within twelve months. Examples of liabilities would be loans, bank overdrafts and trade creditors.

The reason the Accounting Equation works is because every transaction causes the following and therefore has an effect on assets, liabilities or equity:

Increase/decrease in asset balance
Increase/decrease in liability balance
Increase/decrease in Equity

To see how this works in more detail, let's look at the second concept: Double Entry Accounting

Double Entry Accounting

The double entry accounting system simply dictates that 'for every debit, there must be a credit'.

Debits and credits are accounting entries. I will explain this further below, but before we get into that, we need to take a brief look at accounting systems.

'Back in the day', which is an indeterminate point in the past, there were no computerised accounting systems and everything was done on paper. I'm not telling you how old I am, (although you can look me up on LinkedIn and have a guess) but I'm pleased to say I have only ever worked on computerised accounting systems. Having, said that, I did work with some older accountants at the start of my career, who were still using big ledger books, in which they wrote out every transaction for the business they worked for. As you can imagine, this was quite arduous and prone to errors, given the amount of manual entry required.

Nowadays, although everything is computerised, cloud-based, automated and electronic, the fundamental system of recording and reconciling transactions is basically the same.

All accounting systems have a 'Chart of Accounts', also known as the General Ledger (GL) or Nominal Ledger (NL), which is an electronic version of the big books the old accountants used to use. This chart of accounts contains all the accounts required by a specific business. I'm not talking about bank accounts, I mean an account for each transaction type. For example all businesses would need a 'Sales' account, where their customer sales are recorded, but from there it can get very bespoke. A courier business would need an account for 'Fuel' and 'Tyres'. A marketing agency may need accounts for 'Website development' and 'Artwork costs'.

The Chart of Accounts is therefore the root of all transactions. Every single transaction which passes through your business must be posted to an appropriate account. Common accounts in many businesses would be as follows:

Salaries
Computer expenses
Rent
Insurance
Heat and light
Postage
Printing and stationery

Of course there are endless possibilities and some larger businesses would have extremely complex charts of accounts.

As mentioned above, entries are made into these accounts every time the business enters into a new transaction. These entries are always either a debit or a credit.

Debits and credits

NB: This has nothing at all to do with debit cards and credit cards. You may already know that, but it's often been a significant source of confusion when I have explained this concept to people, so I now open with this disclaimer.

Debits and credits are entries into individual accounts within the chart of accounts of a business. A debit entry is posted to the account **receiving** value, while the credit entry is posted to the account **giving** value.

The double entry accounting system dictates that for every debit, there must be a credit. So let's look at how that works in practise.

A simple example would be a cash sale. Let's say your business sells a product for £400. There are no credit terms on the sale, so it's a straight cash sale where you hand over the product and they pay £400 straight into your bank account. The accounting entries for this would be very simple

Debit **Bank**	-	£400
Credit **Sales**	-	£400

The words in bold above represent the names of the accounts in your chart of accounts that would be impacted by this transaction. In this case the **Bank** account has **received** value (£400 cash has been paid in), while the **Sales** account has **given** value (£400 sales have left the business).

Just to address another common source of confusion when I discuss this topic:
In 'real life' when a bank says they've 'credited your account' that means they've put money into it (ie it has received value), but this is because your account is an asset account held by your bank, so while crediting your account increases its value to you, it reduces the value to the bank.

To look at another example, let's say you had to pay for tyres on your company car, which cost £250. Again, there are no credit terms involved, so you have paid the garage straight away when you collected the car. The accounting entries for this would be as follows:

Debit **Vehicle expenses**	-	£250
Credit **Bank**	-	£250

In this case, the expense account (Vehicle expenses) has received value, so it is debited. The bank account has reduced (given value) by £250, so this is a credit entry.

In both of these examples, the important thing to note is that there are **two** entries for every transaction, hence the name 'Double entry system'.

The double entry system is the mechanism by which the Accounting Equation is fulfilled. If every transaction gives rise to two opposing entries of equal value, then assets - liabilities will always equal equity. Earlier in this chapter I said that every transaction would give rise to one of the following:

Increase/decrease in asset balance
Increase/decrease in liability balance
Increase/decrease in Equity

The truth is that every transaction will give rise to **two** of these events, which is what keeps everything in balance.

For example, let's take another look at the two examples above:

Cash sale of £400
This sale gives rise to an increase of £400 in your asset balance (bank account is an asset) and an increase of £400 in sales (and therefore profit), which is an increase in Equity.

Assets   - £400
Liabilities   -   £0
Equity   - £400

Assets - Liabilities = Equity (£400 - £0 = £400)
So the Accounting Equation works

Tyre replacement for £250
This transaction gives rise to an increase in your expenses (a decrease in profit) which is a decrease in Equity, as well as a decrease in your bank balance (an asset).

Assets   - £150 (£400 balance from example 1 -£250)
Liabilities   -   £0 (No liabilities incurred so far)
Equity   - £150 (£400 balance from example 1 -£250)

Assets - Liabilities = Equity (£150 - £0 = £150)
So once again the Accounting Equation works

These are obviously very simple examples, but the point is that the only way the Accounting Equation can be adhered to is because of the Double

Entry accounting system.

Hopefully this makes sense, and this is all the detail we need to go into at this point, because, as stated already, my intention is not to turn my readers into accountants. Having said that, I would certainly encourage you to learn more about this subject and there are massive amounts of resources on the internet for this.

Visibility of Both Sides

The advent of computerised accounting systems has led to some advanced capabilities when it comes to accounting. When transactions were recorded manually on paper, it was eminently possible that someone would make a mistake that would cause the Accounting Equation to fail. Simple things such as dodgy handwriting or poor eyesight could lead to the wrong numbers being written into the wrong column in a book and the Accounting Equation falling down. The resulting errors could take hours, days or weeks to resolve. In some cases they were never resolved and would eventually be written off.

This is no longer possible. A computerised accounting system simply won't allow you to post a transaction unless both sides of the entry agree. Of course other errors are still possible, such as posting a transaction to the wrong account, or entering the wrong amount on both sides, but errors that cause the Accounting Equation to fail won't be permitted by the system.

The Root of Flawless Reliability

The Double Entry system and the Accounting Equation are the main reason for the flawless reliability of Management Accounts, as long as they are done properly. As you've seen in the examples above, everything balances and everything is captured. Every single transaction gives rise to an opposing and equal increase or decrease in assets, liabilities or equity, and therefore the system cannot be fooled. Of course it can be manipulated, but the Four Points of Control framework and the techniques outlined in part two of this book will show you how to minimise corruption and incompetence to create a truly flawless reporting system.

It's now a simple matter to run a Trial Balance (ie a list of all current balances in your Chart of Accounts) from an accounting system at any time, and thanks to the accounting concepts we've looked at so far, and the restrictions imposed by a computerised system, this Trial Balance will always balance, which is to say that the credit balances will always match the debit balances.

To illustrate this, below is a simple example of a Trial Balance

Trial Balance
31st January 2021

Account Ref	Account	Debit - YTD	Credit - YTD
200	Sales Revenue		5,200.00
210	Referral Revenue		4,600.00
416	Depreciation Expense	41.67	
429	General Expenses	103.45	
430	Direct labour	475.00	
441	Legal Expenses	13.00	
463	IT Software and Consumables	231.62	
473	Repairs & Maintenance	88.07	
478	Directors' Remuneration	3,500.00	
489	Telephone & Internet	10.00	
190	Business Bank Account	138.26	
610	Accounts Receivable	5,200.00	
710	Office Equipment	2,299.99	
711	Office Equipment Depreciation		41.67
800	Accounts Payable		1,289.39
835	Directors' Loan Account		1,500.00
980	Owner A Drawings	530.00	
Total		**12,631.06**	**12,631.06**

You don't need to analyse this in detail. The key point is that the debit side and the credit side both agree to the same total - 12,631.06. This must always be the case, no matter the size or complexity of the business.

The Accrual Accounting Convention

The accounting concepts we've looked at so far cover numerical accuracy and balancing. The other concept dealt with in this chapter is the Accrual Accounting Convention, which is concerned with the **timing** of transactions.

The Accrual Accounting Convention is defined as follows:

An accounting system that tries to match the recognition of revenues earned with the expenses incurred in generating those revenues.

It ignores the timing of the cash flows associated with revenues and expenses.

Put simply, it allocates sales revenue and the costs incurred in generating that revenue to the same period.

A vital concept to understand here is the difference between profit and cash flow. The timing of recognising revenue and expenses has nothing to do with the timing of receiving or paying the cash relating to those revenues or expenses.

Why is Timing Important?

There are several reasons why it's important to recognise the timing of revenues and expenses in the correct periods.

Firstly, your performance evaluation can be completely undermined if you inadvertently post transactions into the wrong period. For example, let's say you carry out your performance evaluation and produce your Management Accounts, and it appears that you made a huge profit in the period. Then in the following month you've made far less profit than expected. It then comes to light that a large supplier invoice was accidentally posted into the wrong month. The same could obviously happen with a large sales invoice, with the same overall effect. If this happens, your performance evaluation will have been skewed for two months. This may not be a huge problem as it all comes out in the wash, but what if you had paid bonuses to your team for the month in which you made that huge profit. You can hardly go and ask for it back just because a mistake was made.

Secondly, your profit (and therefore tax) for the year can be incorrectly calculated if you don't capture everything in the correct period. Your statutory accounts must be prepared in accordance with Accounting Standards and this includes the Accrual Accounting Convention. If you don't adhere to these concepts during the year, you may get a nasty surprise at the end of the year, when your accountant decimates your profit by entering accruals for supplier invoices that have not yet been received.

The Accrual Accounting Convention dictates that costs should be recognised in the same period that the revenue generated by those costs is recognised. A simple example of this would be retail stock. For example an e-commerce seller, specialising in dog toys, purchases £50k of stock from China, which arrives in his warehouse on 31st August, accompanied by the invoice, which is dated 20th August. The company paid 50% of the invoice up front, with the balance payable on thirty days terms. So when should this cost be recognised in terms of profit?

Firstly, the payment terms are entirely irrelevant. Whether he paid the whole amount up front, or all of it on thirty days, or £100 per month for the next four years, it has no bearing whatsoever on when the cost is recognised.

The invoice date is usually the trigger. In this case, the invoice will be posted to the system and the date on the invoice (20th August) would normally be the date the cost is recognised. However, since the stock didn't arrive until 31st August, it's unlikely any of it would have been sold in August, so to record a £50k cost, with no sales to offset it, would show a massive loss in the accounts for August. This wouldn't be very good from a Performance Evaluation point of view, as it would show this huge loss, which isn't really a loss. But beyond that, imagine if August was the final month of the company's financial year. This invoice has dropped in just before the end of the year and reduced his profit by £50k. This would significantly reduce his corporation tax for the year. You may say 'so what? There will be an increase in profit the following year, so HMRC will get their tax then'.

Well firstly, that's not the approach HMRC will take and there will be interest (and probably penalties) if this is ever discovered. Of course if they allowed this to stand then all business would time their purchases so that the final month of their year created a massive loss and the tax liabilities were constantly rolling forward into the following year. Secondly, what if there was a change in the corporation tax rate the following year and the business ended up paying more or less tax than they should have if they had done things properly?

So how should this be done? It's fairly simple. The £50k of stock is posted to a **Stock** account, which is held on the balance sheet as a current asset and therefore doesn't touch the P&L. As the stock is sold, the reduction in stock is recognised and matched to the sales revenue, and the cost is recognised at that point. This way, even if the stock is sold months later, the cost is always recognised in the period the revenue is generated. This is one of the reasons a robust stock management system is important in retail.

Stock is a direct cost of sale, so this example shouldn't be hard to understand. However, the same principle applies to all costs in the business, not just the direct costs. Fixed costs such as rent and insurance should also be matched to the periods in which revenue is generated, although you don't need to be quite as precise as you would when it comes to stock and other direct costs.

Accruals and Prepayments

Accruals and prepayments are the mechanisms by which timing issues can be resolved and your accounts can be kept balanced in terms of timing.

An accrual is recognition of a cost which will be incurred in a future period but which relates to the current period.
A prepayment is recognition that a cost incurred in this period actually relates to a future period.

I appreciate that this may a new concept for some readers, but don't worry, we will go through some examples.

Prepayment Example - Annual Insurance Invoice

Below is an example of a full year's P&L for a new company. Pay attention to the 'Insurance' line in the Overheads section.

In this example, the company began in January and had no need for insurance. In April, they decided to take out an insurance policy, for which the premium was £12,000 for the year. The period of insurance was from 1st April 2021 to 31st March 2022. The premium was payable in 10 equal monthly instalments of £1,200 starting in April.

Since the invoice was received in April, it was posted the accounting system in April. The system recognised the invoice date as 1st April and therefore the entire £12,000 invoice was posted to April 2021. As a result, the business made a loss of just under £9,000 in April, despite making a healthy profit every other month so far that year.

By the end of the year, the P&L showed that the business had made a profit every month except April, and that the insurance cost for the year was £12,000, all of which had been incurred in April. Total net profit for the year was £34,224

Monthly P&L 2021

	Jan-21	Feb-21	Mar-21	Apr-21	May-21	Jun-21	Jul-21	Aug-21	Sept-21	Oct-21	Nov-21	Dec-21	YTD
REVENUE													
Sales revenue	13,498	24,344	17,572	15,335	14,461	13,817	21,331	13,099	21,101	20,075	15,624	12,730	202,987
Total Revenue	13,498	24,344	17,572	15,335	14,461	13,817	21,331	13,099	21,101	20,075	15,624	12,730	202,987
COST OF SALES													
Purchases	5,129	9,251	6,677	5,827	5,495	5,250	8,106	4,978	8,018	7,629	5,937	4,837	77,135
Stock movement	945	1,704	1,230	1,073	1,012	967	1,493	917	1,477	1,405	1,094	891	14,209
Direct labour	1,350	2,434	1,757	1,534	1,446	1,382	2,133	1,310	2,110	2,008	1,562	1,273	20,299
Total Cost of Sales	7,424	13,389	9,665	8,434	7,954	7,599	11,732	7,204	11,606	11,041	8,593	7,002	111,643
GROSS PROFIT	6,074	10,955	7,907	6,901	6,507	6,218	9,599	5,895	9,495	9,034	7,031	5,729	91,344
Gross profit percentage	45.0%	45.0%	45.0%	45.0%	45.0%	45.0%	45.0%	45.0%	45.0%	45.0%	45.0%	45.0%	0.0%
OVERHEADS													
Advertising & Marketing	2,000	2,000	2,000	2,000	2,000	2,000	2,000	2,000	2,000	2,000	2,000	2,000	24,000
Staff Salaries	1,500	1,500	1,500	1,500	1,500	1,500	1,500	1,500	1,500	1,500	1,500	1,500	18,000
Computer expenses	50	50	50	50	50	50	50	50	50	50	50	50	600
Insurance	0	0	0	12,000	0	0	0	0	0	0	0	0	12,000
Printing & Stationery	15	15	15	15	15	15	15	15	15	15	15	15	180
Postage	25	25	25	25	25	25	25	25	25	25	25	25	300
Telephone & Internet	50	50	50	50	50	50	50	50	50	50	50	50	600
Premises expenses	120	120	120	120	120	120	120	120	120	120	120	120	1,440
Total Overhead costs	3,760	3,760	3,760	15,760	3,760	3,760	3,760	3,760	3,760	3,760	3,760	3,760	57,120
Net profit	2,314	7,195	4,147	-8,859	2,747	2,458	5,839	2,135	5,735	5,274	3,271	1,969	34,224
Operating profit %age	17.1%	29.6%	23.6%	-57.8%	19.0%	17.8%	27.4%	16.3%	27.2%	26.3%	20.9%	15.5%	16.9%

So let's look at the correct treatment of this insurance invoice, in accordance with the Accrual Accounting Convention.

The ten monthly instalments of £1,200 are entirely irrelevant to the profit calculation, so you can ignore that information.

As mentioned previously, the Accrual Accounting Convention says that costs incurred should be recognised in the same period as the resulting revenues were generated. Although insurance is not a direct cost, it's assumed that all costs in a business contribute to the generation of revenues, even if the contribution is indirect.

Therefore, the cost of the insurance should be attributed to the periods in which it contributes to the generation of revenue. So:

Step 1 - Ascertain in which periods the insurance cost contributes to the generation of revenues.
Step 2 - Apportion the total cost of the insurance to the periods identified in step 1

We know that the insurance cannot have contributed anything in January to March, since the insurance policy was not in force then. We also know that the annual premium, covering twelve months, was £12,000. So £12,000 divided by twelve is £1,000. So:

Step 1 - Periods 4 - 12 (April to December) are the periods in this financial year covered by the insurance policy
Step 2 - The cost per month is £1,000, so this is the cost which should be posted to the **Insurance** account for each month and recognised in the P&L

The correct P&L for this year is therefore shown below:

Monthly P&L 2021

	Jan-21	Feb-21	Mar-21	Apr-21	May-21	Jun-21	Jul-21	Aug-21	Sept-21	Oct-21	Nov-21	Dec-21	YTD
REVENUE													
Sales revenue	13,498	24,344	17,572	15,335	14,461	13,817	21,331	13,099	21,101	20,075	15,624	12,730	202,987
Total Revenue	13,498	24,344	17,572	15,335	14,461	13,817	21,331	13,099	21,101	20,075	15,624	12,730	202,987
COST OF SALES													
Purchases	5,129	9,251	6,677	5,827	5,495	5,250	8,106	4,978	8,018	7,629	5,937	4,837	77,135
Stock movement	945	1,704	1,230	1,073	1,012	967	1,493	917	1,477	1,405	1,094	891	14,209
Direct labour	1,350	2,434	1,757	1,534	1,446	1,382	2,133	1,310	2,110	2,008	1,562	1,273	20,299
Total Cost of Sales	7,424	13,389	9,665	8,434	7,954	7,599	11,732	7,204	11,606	11,041	8,593	7,002	111,643
GROSS PROFIT	6,074	10,955	7,907	6,901	6,507	6,218	9,599	5,895	9,495	9,034	7,031	5,729	91,344
Gross profit percentage	45.0%	45.0%	45.0%	45.0%	45.0%	45.0%	45.0%	45.0%	45.0%	45.0%	45.0%	45.0%	0.0%
OVERHEADS													
Advertising & Marketing	2,000	2,000	2,000	2,000	2,000	2,000	2,000	2,000	2,000	2,000	2,000	2,000	24,000
Staff Salaries	1,500	1,500	1,500	1,500	1,500	1,500	1,500	1,500	1,500	1,500	1,500	1,500	18,000
Computer expenses	50	50	50	50	50	50	50	50	50	50	50	50	600
Insurance	0	0	0	12,000	0	0	0	0	0	0	0	0	12,000
Printing & Stationery	15	15	15	15	15	15	15	15	15	15	15	15	180
Postage	25	25	25	25	25	25	25	25	25	25	25	25	300
Telephone & Internet	50	50	50	50	50	50	50	50	50	50	50	50	600
Premises expenses	120	120	120	120	120	120	120	120	120	120	120	120	1,440
Total Overhead costs	3,760	3,760	3,760	15,760	3,760	3,760	3,760	3,760	3,760	3,760	3,760	3,760	57,120
Net profit	2,314	7,195	4,147	-8,859	2,747	2,458	5,839	2,135	5,735	5,274	3,271	1,969	34,224
Operating profit %age	17.1%	29.6%	23.6%	-57.8%	19.0%	17.8%	27.4%	16.3%	27.2%	26.3%	20.9%	15.5%	16.9%

There are a several things to note in this version.

1. The insurance cost for each month from April onwards now shows as £1,000 per month.
2. This means the £9k loss in April has become a £2k profit and all subsequent months are showing £1k less profit than they did in the previous (incorrect) version.
3. The total Insurance cost for the year is now £9k, as opposed to £12k. This is because the insurance policy actually covers the period until March 2022. The remaining three months of £1,000 cost will appear in next year's P&L in January, February and March
4. The £3k reduction in Insurance cost means a £3k increase in profit for the year. This is important to get right, from a performance evaluation point of view, as well as the corporation tax implications.

So this is how Prepayments work. Now let's look at the opposite of a Prepayment, an Accrual.

Accrual Example - Electricity Bill

Accruals are less likely than Prepayments to cover long periods. Annual or quarterly invoices are usually received (and dated) at the start of the charging period. It's very unusual that you will receive an invoice at the end of a charging period, unless it's a fairly short charging period. For that reason, Accruals are usually for shorter periods, such as a month or a few weeks.

A typical example of this would be an electricity bill, since it can't be generated until the end of the period in which the electricity has been used.

In the example below, if you focus on the 'Electricity cost' line in the overheads section, you will see that from January to April, the electricity cost was posted with no problems. In May, there was no electricity cost at all and then in June the cost was roughly double the average charge from previous months.

It's possible that the business was closed in May and incurred no electricity cost, which would be perfectly acceptable from an accounting point of view, but £14k of revenue has been recognised in May, so this was obviously not the case. In actuality, the electricity bill was received late and posted into June, hence the relatively high cost in June.

This doesn't present a huge problem. Unlike the Insurance example, which was for a large sum of money, this is around £500 and is caught up in the following month, so no harm done, let's just get on with our lives, right?

Well, bear in mind that this is just a simple example in a book using a small set of accounts and relatively insignificant figures. In reality, a business may have multiple accounts which are subject to timing delays, so it's important to get these processes in place, regardless of the amounts. You may say that HMRC won't care about this one, since everything catches up a month later and the annual profit is unaffected. This is true, but now look at December, where the same thing has apparently happened and the electricity bill has slipped into January of the following year.

So how should this be dealt with?

Monthly P&L 2021

	Jan-21	Feb-21	Mar-21	Apr-21	May-21	Jun-21	Jul-21	Aug-21	Sept-21	Oct-21	Nov-21	Dec-21	YTD
REVENUE													
Sales revenue	13,498	24,344	17,572	15,335	14,461	13,817	21,331	13,099	21,101	20,075	15,624	12,730	202,987
Total Revenue	13,498	24,344	17,572	15,335	14,461	13,817	21,331	13,099	21,101	20,075	15,624	12,730	202,987
COST OF SALES													
Purchases	5,129	9,251	6,677	5,827	5,495	5,250	8,106	4,978	8,018	7,629	5,937	4,837	77,135
Stock movement	945	1,704	1,230	1,073	1,012	967	1,493	917	1,477	1,405	1,094	891	14,209
Direct labour	1,350	2,434	1,757	1,534	1,446	1,382	2,133	1,310	2,110	2,008	1,562	1,273	20,299
Total Cost of Sales	7,424	13,389	9,665	8,434	7,954	7,599	11,732	7,204	11,606	11,041	8,593	7,002	111,643
GROSS PROFIT	6,074	10,955	7,907	6,901	6,507	6,218	9,599	5,895	9,495	9,034	7,031	5,729	91,344
Gross profit percentage	45.0%	45.0%	45.0%	45.0%	45.0%	45.0%	45.0%	45.0%	45.0%	45.0%	45.0%	45.0%	0.0%
OVERHEADS													
Advertising & Marketing	2,000	2,000	2,000	2,000	2,000	2,000	2,000	2,000	2,000	2,000	2,000	2,000	24,000
Staff Salaries	1,500	1,500	1,500	1,500	1,500	1,500	1,500	1,500	1,500	1,500	1,500	1,500	18,000
Computer expenses	50	50	50	50	50	50	50	50	50	50	50	50	600
Electricity cost	616	438	610	586	0	1,042	381	559	451	625	586	0	5,894
Printing & Stationery	15	15	15	15	15	15	15	15	15	15	15	15	180
Postage	25	25	25	25	25	25	25	25	25	25	25	25	300
Telephone & Internet	50	50	50	50	50	50	50	50	50	50	50	50	600
Premises expenses	120	120	120	120	120	120	120	120	120	120	120	120	1,440
Total Overhead costs	4,376	4,198	4,370	4,346	3,760	4,802	4,141	4,319	4,211	4,385	4,346	3,760	51,014
Net profit	1,698	6,757	3,537	2,555	2,747	1,416	5,458	1,576	5,284	4,649	2,685	1,969	40,330
Operating profit %age	12.6%	27.8%	20.1%	16.7%	19.0%	10.2%	25.6%	12.0%	25.0%	23.2%	17.2%	15.5%	19.9%

Unlike prepayments, where the figures have been invoiced in advance and are therefore known, accruals will often have to be estimates or averages. In this case, you may be able to contact the electricity company and ask for a figure to accrue. Failing that, you can look at the energy cost in the same month in previous years and how it relates to this year. For example if last year we used 20% more energy in May than we did in April and there's no reason to suspect this year will be different, you can calculate an accrual from the April expense.

The 'correct' approach is illustrated on the next page:

Monthly P&L 2021

	Jan-21	Feb-21	Mar-21	Apr-21	May-21	Jun-21	Jul-21	Aug-21	Sept-21	Oct-21	Nov-21	Dec-21	YTD
REVENUE													
Sales revenue	13,498	24,344	17,572	15,335	14,461	13,817	21,331	13,099	21,101	20,075	15,624	12,730	202,987
Total Revenue	13,498	24,344	17,572	15,335	14,461	13,817	21,331	13,099	21,101	20,075	15,624	12,730	202,987
COST OF SALES													
Purchases	5,129	9,251	6,677	5,827	5,495	5,250	8,106	4,978	8,018	7,629	5,937	4,837	77,135
Stock movement	945	1,704	1,230	1,073	1,012	967	1,493	917	1,477	1,405	1,094	891	14,209
Direct labour	1,350	2,434	1,757	1,534	1,446	1,382	2,133	1,310	2,110	2,008	1,562	1,273	20,299
Total Cost of Sales	7,424	13,389	9,665	8,434	7,954	7,599	11,732	7,204	11,606	11,041	8,593	7,002	111,643
GROSS PROFIT	6,074	10,955	7,907	6,901	6,507	6,218	9,599	5,895	9,495	9,034	7,031	5,729	91,344
Gross profit percentage	45.0%	45.0%	45.0%	45.0%	45.0%	45.0%	45.0%	45.0%	45.0%	45.0%	45.0%	45.0%	0.0%
OVERHEADS													
Advertising & Marketing	2,000	2,000	2,000	2,000	2,000	2,000	2,000	2,000	2,000	2,000	2,000	2,000	24,000
Staff Salaries	1,500	1,500	1,500	1,500	1,500	1,500	1,500	1,500	1,500	1,500	1,500	1,500	18,000
Computer expenses	50	50	50	50	50	50	50	50	50	50	50	50	600
Electricity cost	616	438	610	586	464	578	381	559	451	625	586	570	6,464
Printing & Stationery	15	15	15	15	15	15	15	15	15	15	15	15	180
Postage	25	25	25	25	25	25	25	25	25	25	25	25	300
Telephone & Internet	50	50	50	50	50	50	50	50	50	50	50	50	600
Premises expenses	120	120	120	120	120	120	120	120	120	120	120	120	1,440
Total Overhead costs	4,376	4,198	4,370	4,346	4,224	4,338	4,141	4,319	4,211	4,385	4,346	4,330	51,584
Net profit	1,698	6,757	3,537	2,555	2,283	1,880	5,458	1,576	5,284	4,649	2,685	1,399	39,760
Operating profit %age	12.6%	27.8%	20.1%	16.7%	15.8%	13.6%	25.6%	12.0%	25.0%	23.2%	17.2%	11.0%	19.6%

In this version, you can see that an accrual has been entered in both May and December. This has resulted in more accurate cost/profit figures for each month and the total profit for the year is now correct.

Where are Accruals and Prepayment 'Kept'

You may be wondering, especially after my explanation of the double entry system, how accruals and prepayments are managed from an accounting point of view.

A business will usually have multiple prepayments and accruals running throughout their financial year, so the balances are retained on the Balance Sheet until everything reverses itself out again. The Prepayments balance is recognised as an asset, while the Accruals balance is recognised as a liability, the logic being that we have an unpaid debt to the energy company, even if we haven't actually received the bill yet.

It may help to think of these items as similar to the stock balance I referred to earlier. Insurance is not a stock item, obviously, but if you think of it that you have purchased twelve 'units' of insurance, which you are holding in stock and will be 'selling' them off monthly, you wouldn't be that far from the accounting theory.

Accounting Concepts - A Summary

As mentioned previously in this chapter, it's vital you understand these concepts so that you can, at least, understand the information and reporting produced by your accountant or FD but, ideally, so that you can produce accurate and meaningful Performance Evaluation.

The Double Entry system and the Accounting Equation will ensure that every transaction in your business is picked up in your Management Accounts. The Accrual Accounting Convention will ensure that it all appears in the correct period. Once you have these elements covered, you are well on your way to producing flawlessly reliable reporting that will drive your business forwards and maximise your profitable growth.

Chapter 7 - Performance Evaluation

The Three Elements of Control

When a business fails, by which I mean completely ceases trading due to financial failure, there may be several reasons. However, those reasons will ultimately be attributable to one or more of the elements of control referred to in the Control Cycle: Performance Evaluation, Economic Viability and Compliance. Conversely then, it stands to reason that if you establish and maintain those elements of control, your business will not fail.

These elements of control are so comprehensive that they will pinpoint the exact actions required to achieve success in your business. If success is unachievable because the business is not economically viable, the Control Cycle will flush out the reasons for this, so that you can then determine what action is required to make it viable. If this is impossible, you may be forced to conclude that the business simply isn't a viable venture and pursue something else instead. This may seem like a failure, but acknowledging this before you remortgage your house or cause collateral damage to other businesses/ livelihoods is still a preferable outcome.

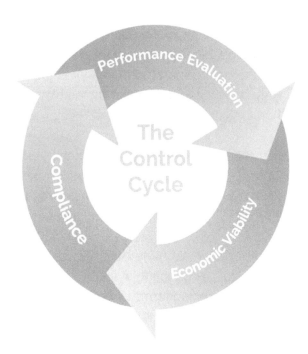

Performance Evaluation

The first and most important step in the Control Cycle is Performance Evaluation. The reason this comes first is because it's impossible to ascertain your economic viability without first evaluating your performance.

The meaning of Performance Evaluation in this context is 'How are we doing?'. This is very different to 'How did we do?', which is the only perspective offered by your year-end accounts.

Performance Review vs Performance Evaluation

Reporting regulations in the UK dictate that businesses must report their financial statements publicly within nine months of their financial year end. Until this point, there is no obligation to carry out or document any kind of evaluation or performance review.

This means that many businesses have no real clue as to how their business has performed until well after the year has ended. When they receive their statutory accounts from their accountant, the period under review has now ended and can't be influenced.

Performance Evaluation asks '*How are we doing?*' as opposed to '*How did we do?*'. This seems like a subtle distinction but it makes a huge difference. Because it's carried out periodically throughout the year, instead of at the end of the year, you can use the data generated to influence the eventual outcome. This is infinitely better than just letting things play out and making decisions on the fly, then looking backwards at the result.

Reviewing your performance several months after the year has ended is not performance evaluation. True performance evaluation needs to be undertaken during the year and it needs to be flawlessly reliable. There is only one way to achieve this - monthly Management Accounts.

Of course, there are other evaluation methods. Score-cards, sales reports, profit and loss reports from your accounting system etc all have their place but none of them are flawlessly reliable in terms of numerical accuracy and timing. Furthermore, none of them mirror the conditions and standards that will be applied to your statutory accounts.

Flawless Reliability

To achieve flawless reliability, Performance Evaluation needs to feature the following controls:

1. Prepared in accordance with the accounting concepts described in the previous chapter.
2. Comparative reporting against an annual budget and historical results.

The comparatives referred to in point two above also contribute to the evaluation process and ultimately determine the economic viability of your business. This is how we answer the question *"How are we doing?"* with objective evidence.

Budgeting

A budget is one of the most important documents a business can produce. I would even go as far as to say that without a budget, profitable growth is pretty much impossible, except by accident.

Despite this, many of the clients I work with don't have a budget in place until they start working with us. Even then, they often don't really understand the purpose or the point until months later, when they see it in action.

Budgeting is too big and complex a subject to address in this book and actually warrants a book of its own, but I will explain the fundamental points here.

A commercial budget differs considerably from a household budget, which is the type of budget most people think of when they hear the word 'budget'. A household budget is designed to restrict spending because the level of income is usually finite and spending beyond this level leads to problems.

A commercial budget is completely different. The focus is not on restriction but on optimisation of resources to increase income and maximise profit. The budget should be the most realistic expectation of the revenues achievable using the assets and resources available to the business.

The key words in this definition are 'realistic' and 'expectation'. A budget should not be the best-case or worst-case scenario, it should be the most-likely-case scenario.

Just as Management Accounts are not Management Accounts without a budget, a budget is largely pointless without Management Accounts. If you create a budget at the beginning of the year and then forget about it until the end of the year, you have slipped back into the '*How did we do?*' mindset.

The real purpose and benefit of a commercial budget is that you have a benchmark for each month and the current year to date. At the end of each period you produce your Management Accounts and measure the key performance indicators against your budget. In this context, the question '*How are we doing?*' suddenly becomes a simple matter of mathematics. If you're meeting or exceeding your budgeted figures, you're doing well. If not, you need to understand why and make some changes - **during** the year.

This is really the crux of what we're talking about. The main benefit of Performance Evaluation is that, rather than waiting until the end of the year to review your accounts and see how you did, you evaluate your performance monthly, make data-driven decisions and take control of how you're doing.

Prior Year Comparison

The other key comparator in your Management Accounts is the same month for the previous year. This is less important than reviewing against your budget, but it can provide useful historical comparisons, especially when the focus of the business is growth. Reviewing against historical data is useful when drilling into the detail. For example, it may be useful to examine changes in customer base and product mix from one year to the next.

Management Accounts

So, what are Management Accounts? If you're experienced in business, you may already know. However, I have worked with a number of different sized business, in a variety of sectors, who either don't know what Management Accounts consist of. Many times I have started working with a client and asked to see their Management Accounts, only to be presented with a document which is definitely **not** Management Accounts.

Management Accounts are an internal document, meant for review by the leaders of the business to enable performance evaluation and support decision-making within the business. 'Internal' in this sense means they are used internally, not necessarily produced internally, although producing them in-house is, in my experience, far more preferable to outsourcing them.

Your accountant would, of course, be quite happy to produce your accounts monthly instead of annually, but this would end up being very expensive.

A far better approach is to bring this process in-house and run it monthly. Naturally, this would be less expensive than paying an accountant to do it, but there are several other benefits:

- Accuracy - Producing accounts monthly means that anomalies are investigated at the time and questions are answered promptly. This is far better than looking back a year later and trying to remember what happened.
- Cost - Monthly accounts x 12 = annual accounts. Producing accurate and consistent monthly accounts means you can simply hand over your Management Accounts to your accountant for review, conclusion and filing. This should reduce their bill considerably.
- Awareness - The greatest benefit of all. As a business owner, reviewing your accounts on a monthly basis would give you the insight and data to fully understand every element of your business and make timely and impactful decisions.

The purpose of Management Accounts is to provide adequate data to the controllers of a business to enable them to fulfil their responsibilities as directors.

Essentially, Management Accounts are a diagnostic tool used to quickly and easily identify areas of success and failure, so that greater scrutiny can be applied to those areas in order to maximise the successes and minimise the failures, thereby making the company successful. This 'greater scrutiny' comes in the form of focused reporting and analysis.

To summarise, monthly Management Accounts, if prepared correctly, provide flawless Performance Evaluation, enabling you to assess your Economic Viability. However, this is only the case if they feature the following characteristics:

- Comparative reporting against the budgeted performance for the period
- Comparative reporting against the equivalent period in the previous year
- Adherence to the three accounting concepts outlined in the previous chapter
- Produced and presented monthly, regardless of business output or activity
- Produced in a timely manner, so that decisions can be made as soon as possible
- Consistent application of techniques and processes

Financial statements

Adherence to accounting principles also means that Management Accounts must be a full set of financial statements, not just a profit and loss report (P&L). They must include a Profit and Loss Report, a Balance Sheet and a Cash Flow Statement as a **minimum.** A full set of Management Accounts (often known as a 'board pack') may include all manner of additional supporting reports or even independent reports, such as stock listings, sales performance, non-financial KPIs, HR reporting or anything else, but the three financial statements and shown below must be the core documents.

Profit & Loss Report (P&L) - The results for the period

PROFIT & LOSS - JANUARY 2021							
	Actual January		Budget January		Variance	Prior year January		Variance

	Actual January		Budget January		Variance	Prior year January		Variance
REVENUE								
Transport Income	267,025		265,000		2,025	178,223		88,802
Other Income	0		0		0	0		0
Total Revenue	267,025		265,000		2,025	178,223		88,802
COST OF SALES								
Direct Labour	27,233	10.2%	27,000	10.2%	(233)	19,066	10.7%	(8,167)
Fuel	53,405	20.0%	55,000	20.8%	1,595	38,839	21.8%	(14,566)
Fleet Maintenance	7,600	2.8%	7,500	2.8%	(100)	5,296	3.0%	(2,304)
Subcontractors	3,819	1.4%	4,000	1.5%	181	2,825	1.6%	(994)
Fleet Insurances	9,120	3.4%	9,000	3.4%	(120)	6,355	3.6%	(2,765)
Tyres	3,230	1.2%	3,500	1.3%	270	2,472	1.4%	(758)
Operators & Vehicle Licences	950	0.4%	1,000	0.4%	50	706	0.4%	(244)
Total Cost of Sales	105,357	39.5%	107,000	40.4%	1,643	75,560	42.4%	(29,797)
GROSS PROFIT	161,668		158,000		3,668	102,663		118,599
Gross profit margin	60.5%		59.6%			57.6%		133.6%
OVERHEADS								
Administrative Salaries	63,540	23.8%	63,500	24.0%	(40)	44,842	25.2%	(18,698)
Insurances	19,322	7.2%	19,750	7.5%	428	13,947	7.8%	(5,375)
Accountancy & Audit fees	9,042	3.4%	9,000	3.4%	(42)	6,355	3.6%	(2,687)
Bank Charges	950	0.4%	1,000	0.4%	50	706	0.4%	(244)
Legal & Professional	7,490	2.8%	7,500	2.8%	10	5,296	3.0%	(2,194)
Printing & Stationery	2,075	0.8%	2,000	0.8%	(75)	1,412	0.8%	(662)
Telephone & Internet	3,425	1.3%	3,500	1.3%	75	2,472	1.4%	(953)
Training	4,950	1.9%	5,000	1.9%	50	3,531	2.0%	(1,419)
Depreciation	13,300	5.0%	13,000	4.9%	(300)	9,180	5.2%	(4,120)
Computer Expenses	2,491	0.9%	2,500	0.9%	9	1,765	1.0%	(726)
Subsistence	3,230	1.2%	3,000	1.1%	(230)	2,118	1.2%	(1,112)
Uniforms & Protective Clothing	2,533	0.9%	2,500	0.9%	(33)	1,765	1.0%	(767)
Advertising & Promotional Costs	10,827	4.1%	11,000	4.2%	173	7,768	4.4%	(3,060)
Health & Safety	1,950	0.7%	2,000	0.8%	50	1,412	0.8%	(538)
Total Overhead costs	145,125	54.3%	145,250	54.8%	125	102,571	57.6%	(42,554)
Overhead %age	54.3%		54.8%			57.6%		
Total Overheads & Cost of Sales	250,482	93.8%	252,250	95.2%	1,768	178,131	99.9%	(72,351)
Net Profit	16,543	6.2%	12,750	4.8%	3,793	92	0.1%	16,451
Net profit margin	6.2%		4.8%			0.1%		

The P&L (also known as the Income Statement) is a record of the results achieved in the period. For maximum effectiveness, monthly Management Accounts should actually include two P&Ls. One for the period being reported on in isolation and one showing the cumulative results for the year. This approach shows how we performed in the month, but also how we are progressing against the annual budget.

It's important to understand that the P&L only shows the results for the period to which it relates, and historical results are omitted. For example the P&L for April will not show the results for March, even if they are part of the same financial year. Historical data is consolidated in your Balance Sheet.

The Balance Sheet - Cumulative balances from day one

Balance Sheet: January 2021	Jan-21
Fixed Assets	
Fixed assets - Office Equipment	3,582
Fixed assets - Plant & Machinery	14,856
Fixed assets - Motor Vehicles	9,855
Total Fixed Assts	28,293
Current Assets	
Accounts Receivable	27,856
Bank & cash Equivalents	42,887
Prepayments	5,246
Other current assets	452
Total Current Assets	76,441
Current Liabilities	
Accounts Payable	18,542
Accruals	11,244
PAYE Payable	2,585
VAT Liability	8,542
Pension contributions payable	845
Other current liabilities	642
Total Current Liabilities	42,400
Long Term Liabilities	
Loans	8,528
Hire purchase	1,419
Total Long Term Liabilities	9,947
NET ASSETS	52,387
Funded by:	
Share Capital	100
Current year profit	16,543
Retained Earnings	35,744
Dividends	0
EQUITY	52,387

Unlike the P&L, the Balance Sheet accumulates balances of all transactions from the day your business began. Whereas the P&L keeps track of transactions in the period under review, the Balance Sheet keeps track of assets and liabilities for as long as they exist. For example if you create a savings account the day you start your business and deposit £10k into that account, it will remain there as an asset until you withdraw it, even if that's twenty years later.

As outlined in the previous chapter, according to the Accounting Equation, every transaction in your business will cause at least one of the following and therefore has an effect on assets, liabilities or equity:

Increase/decrease in asset balance
Increase/decrease in liability balance
Increase/decrease in Equity

As we will explore later in this chapter, the Balance sheet provides the 'anchor' for your Management Accounts and is the root of the aforementioned flawless reliability.

The Cash Flow Statement - Liquidity and cash utilisation

Cash flow statement	Jan-21
Receipts:	
Sales receipts	196,523
Interest received	104
Total:	196,627
Payments:	
Accountancy/Audit	-
Computer/IT charges	2,539
Dividends	-
Legal/Professional	257
Loan repayments	650
Marketing/Advertising	5,288
Mobile phones	1,285
Rent/Rates	4,285
Repair/Maintenance	129
Space rental	73
Statutory payments/HMRC	37,511
Subsistence	1,706
Sundry expenses	103
Telephone/Broadband	10
Utilities	2,452
Wages/Salaries	119,539
Waste management	502
	176,329
Nett Cashflow/(Outflow)	20,298
Opening balance	22,589
Cash Movement	20,298
Closing balance	42,887

The cash flow statement is the final piece of the puzzle as far as Management Accounts are concerned. Control of cash in business is absolutely vital and even highly profitable businesses can fail if their cash is tied up in stock/assets and they are unable to pay their bills as they fall due.

It's important to remember that the Accrual Accounting Convention (skip back to the previous chapter if you need a refresher of this concept) completely ignores the timing of cash flows when determining profit, which is why a profitable business can still fail if they don't keep tabs on their cash flow. This was demonstrated in the insurance example in the previous chapter, where £12,000 was payable to the insurance company in one month, even though the cost was spread across the year at £1,000 per month.

You should also consider that a business will have cash obligations which are completely outside of any profit calculations. For example VAT and loan repayments. VAT-registered business are obliged to add VAT to their sales invoices and collect this on behalf of HMRC. However, collection of VAT is not sales revenue and payment of VAT is not an expense.

Similarly, receipt of a loan advance is not sales revenue and the loan repayments are not considered an expense. These are also ignored by the P&L of a business (apart from the interest charged, which is a legitimate expense).

This is an important concept to understand. Cash may be payable from your bank account regardless of the profit generated. If you have a record month in terms of sales and profit, but none of those customers have yet paid, and in the meantime you have a huge VAT bill to pay, or a large loan repayment, this is where cash 'bottlenecks' can occur and cause serious problems in a business.

How is 'Flawless Reliability' Achieved

The reason all three of these documents **must** be included in your Management Accounts is to ensure the flawless reliability I keep talking about.

Every transaction in your business is captured in the P&L in the month it occurs and gives rise to either an asset or a liability in the Balance Sheet. These assets and liabilities will eventually be settled in cash and recorded in your Cash Flow Statement.

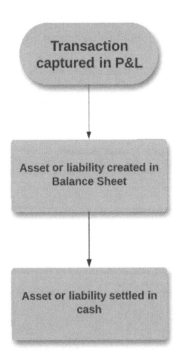

This means that every transaction your business engages in will be at some point of the above transition at any given moment. By pulling them all together, nothing can be missed and the reconciliation techniques described in the second part of this book ensure that no errors can be made. The result of this is flawless Performance Evaluation, which enables the assessment of your Economic Viability and from there we can look at Compliance, to complete the Control Cycle.

'Anchoring' Your Accounts

So in practical terms, how do the Management Accounts ensure that everything has been captured.

Ultimately, the key is the Balance Sheet, which is why it's such a vital part of the Management Accounts pack. The Balance Sheet pulls together the balances of all assets and liabilities in the business and compares them to the Equity held in the business. If you recall the Accounting Equation presented in the previous chapter:

Equity = (Assets - Liabilities)

So, fundamentally, the balance of the net assets (ie the assets - the liabilities) of the business must equal the equity. The Balance Sheet proves that this is the case. If we revisit the example we looked at earlier, this will make more sense.

Balance Sheet: January 2021	Jan-21
Fixed Assets	
Fixed assets - Office Equipment	3,582
Fixed assets - Plant & Machinery	14,856
Fixed assets - Motor Vehicles	9,855
Total Fixed Assts	28,293
Current Assets	
Accounts Receivable	27,856
Bank & cash Equivalents	42,887
Prepayments	5,246
Other current assets	452
Total Current Assets	76,441
Current Liabilities	
Accounts Payable	18,542
Accruals	11,244
PAYE Payable	2,585
VAT Liability	8,542
Pension contributions payable	845
Other current liabilities	642
Total Current Liabilities	42,400
Long Term Liabilities	
Loans	8,528
Hire purchase	1,419
Total Long Term Liabilities	9,947
NET ASSETS	52,387
Funded by:	
Share Capital	100
Current year profit	16,543
Retained Earnings	35,744
Dividends	0
EQUITY	52,387

As you can see from the sections highlighted red, the net assets do indeed balance with the equity and the Accounting Equation is satisfied.

The theory behind the Accounting Equation is that every asset is financed either by a liability or the reduction of another asset, which must always be the case. For example if you purchase a forklift, which is an asset, for £70k and pay for it from your bank account, you would increase the value of your fixed assets by £70k, while reducing your bank balance (another asset) by £70k. The net movement is zero. You have essentially just swapped one £70k asset for another £70k asset.

If you purchase the same forklift using a bank loan, you would increase the value of your fixed assets by £70k, but you would also recognise a £70k liability for the loan, so again, the net movement is zero. Of course the loan would probably give rise to interest charges, which would be an expense and therefore reduce profit.

So if the interest on the loan was £5k, this would be recognised as a liability, so profit (Equity) would be reduced by £5k, so the Net Assets would still agree with the Equity.

But so what? This is just an Excel sheet. I could have just typed those numbers in to make it agree, right?

In theory that's true, but let's compare the Balance Sheet to the P&L.

PROFIT & LOSS - JANUARY 2021

	Actual January	Budget January	Variance	Prior year January	Variance
REVENUE					
Transport Income	267,025	265,000	2,025	178,223	88,802
Other Income	0	0	0	0	0
Total Revenue	267,025	265,000	2,025	178,223	88,802
COST OF SALES					
Direct Labour	27,233 10.2%	27,000 10.2%	(233)	19,066 10.7%	(8,167)
Fuel	53,405 20.0%	55,000 20.8%	1,595	38,839 21.8%	(14,566)
Fleet Maintenance	7,600 2.8%	7,500 2.8%	(100)	5,296 3.0%	(2,304)
Subcontractors	3,819 1.4%	4,000 1.5%	181	2,825 1.6%	(994)
Fleet Insurances	9,120 3.4%	9,000 3.4%	(120)	6,355 3.6%	(2,765)
Tyres	3,230 1.2%	3,500 1.3%	270	2,472 1.4%	(758)
Operators & Vehicle Licences	950 0.4%	1,000 0.4%	50	706 0.4%	(244)
Total Cost of Sales	105,357 39.5%	107,000 40.4%	1,643	75,560 42.4%	(29,797)
GROSS PROFIT	161,668	158,000	3,668	102,663	118,599
Gross profit margin	60.5%	59.6%		57.6%	133.6%
OVERHEADS					
Administrative Salaries	63,540 23.8%	63,500 24.0%	(40)	44,842 25.2%	(18,698)
Insurances	19,322 7.2%	19,750 7.5%	428	13,947 7.8%	(5,375)
Accountancy & Audit fees	9,042 3.4%	9,000 3.4%	(42)	6,355 3.6%	(2,687)
Bank Charges	950 0.4%	1,000 0.4%	50	706 0.4%	(244)
Legal & Professional	7,490 2.8%	7,500 2.8%	10	5,296 3.0%	(2,194)
Printing & Stationery	2,075 0.8%	2,000 0.8%	(75)	1,412 0.8%	(662)
Telephone & Internet	3,425 1.3%	3,500 1.3%	75	2,472 1.4%	(953)
Training	4,950 1.9%	5,000 1.9%	50	3,531 2.0%	(1,419)
Depreciation	13,300 5.0%	13,000 4.9%	(300)	9,180 5.2%	(4,120)
Computer Expenses	2,491 0.9%	2,500 0.9%	9	1,765 1.0%	(726)
Subsistence	3,230 1.2%	3,000 1.1%	(230)	2,118 1.2%	(1,112)
Uniforms & Protective Clothing	2,533 0.9%	2,500 0.9%	(33)	1,765 1.0%	(767)
Advertising & Promotional Costs	10,827 4.1%	11,000 4.2%	173	7,768 4.4%	(3,060)
Health & Safety	1,950 0.7%	2,000 0.8%	50	1,412 0.8%	(538)
Total Overhead costs	145,125 54.3%	145,250 54.8%	125	102,571 57.6%	(42,554)
Overhead %age	54.3%	54.8%		57.6%	
Total Overheads & Cost of Sales	250,482 93.8%	252,250 95.2%	1,768	178,131 99.9%	(72,351)
Net Profit	16,543 6.2%	12,750 4.8%	3,793	92 0.1%	16,451
Net profit margin	6.2%	4.8%		0.1%	

Balance Sheet: January 2021	Jan-21
Fixed Assets	
Fixed assets - Office Equipment	3,582
Fixed assets - Plant & Machinery	14,856
Fixed assets - Motor Vehicles	9,855
Total Fixed Assts	28,293
Current Assets	
Accounts Receivable	27,856
Bank & cash Equivalents	42,887
Prepayments	5,246
Other current assets	452
Total Current Assets	76,441
Current Liabilities	
Accounts Payable	18,542
Accruals	11,244
PAYE Payable	2,585
VAT Liability	8,542
Pension contributions payable	845
Other current liabilities	642
Total Current Liabilities	42,400
Long Term Liabilities	
Loans	8,528
Hire purchase	1,419
Total Long Term Liabilities	9,947
NET ASSETS	**52,387**
Funded by:	
Share Capital	
Current year profit	**16,543**
Retained Earnings	
Dividends	
EQUITY	**52,387**

You can now see that the 'Current year profit' figure in the Balance Sheet is taken from the P&L. If this number was anything other than £16,543, then the total Equity would no longer be £52,387 and would therefore not agree to the Net Assets, causing the Accounting Equation to fail.

Of course I could still be fiddling it by tweaking the numbers on the P&L to force them to total £16,543 but as part of the Management Accounts process, every number on the P&L would have been reconciled to an independent document (as described in Part Two of this book). Apart from that, it would be a simple matter to run a report from the accounting system to prove the balances if there was any suspicion of dishonesty or incompetence.

So we've now examined the link between the Balance Sheet and the P&L, but there is a third piece of this puzzle. The Cash Flow Statement.

Balance Sheet: January 2021	Jan-21
Fixed Assets	
Fixed assets - Office Equipment	3,582
Fixed assets - Plant & Machinery	14,856
Fixed assets - Motor Vehicles	9,855
Total Fixed Assts	28,293
Current Assets	
Accounts Receivable	27,856
Bank & cash Equivalents	42,887
Prepayments	5,246
Other current assets	452
Total Current Assets	76,441
Current Liabilities	
Accounts Payable	18,542
Accruals	11,244
PAYE Payable	2,585
VAT Liability	8,542
Pension contributions payable	845
Other current liabilities	642
Total Current Liabilities	42,400
Long Term Liabilities	
Loans	8,528
Hire purchase	1,419
Total Long Term Liabilities	9,947
NET ASSETS	52,387
Funded by:	
Share Capital	
Current year profit	16,543
Retained Earnings	35,744
Dividends	0
EQUITY	52,387

Cash flow statement	Jan-21
Receipts:	
Sales receipts	196,523
Interest received	104
Total:	196,627
Payments:	
Accountancy/Audit	-
Computer/IT charges	2,539
Dividends	-
Legal/Professional	257
Loan repayments	650
Marketing/Advertising	5,288
Mobile phones	1,285
Rent/Rates	4,285
Repair/Maintenance	129
Space rental	73
Statutory payments/HMRC	37,511
Subsistence	1,706
Sundry expenses	103
Telephone/Broadband	10
Utilities	2,452
Wages/Salaries	119,539
Waste management	502
	176,329
Nett Cashflow/(Outflow)	20,298
Opening balance	22,589
Cash Movement	20,298
Closing balance	42,887

As mentioned previously, the Balance Sheet compiles and presents the cumulative balances of all assets and liabilities within the business, including the cash balances. As you can see from the highlighted figures above, the Closing Balance from the Cash Flow Statement is £42,887, which is reflected in the Current Assets section of the Balance Sheet. Once again, if this was anything other than £42,887, the Net Assets would not be £52,387 and the Accounting Equation would fail.

It's important to recognise that the flawless reliability achieved by Management Accounts is contingent on the data and processes used to create them. As with any system, if you put rubbish in, you will get rubbish out. You will need to implement the processes in Part Two of this book to ensure that your accounting system is managed properly, your input data is accurate and that steps are taken to limit corruption and incompetence in your organisation. But with these caveats aside, Management Accounts, unlike any other business reporting framework, are infallible if done right.

Comparative Reporting

	PROFIT & LOSS - JANUARY 2021
	Actual January
REVENUE	
Transport Income	267,025
Other Income	0
Total Revenue	267,025
COST OF SALES	
Direct Labour	27,233 10.2%
Fuel	53,405 20.0%
Fleet Maintenance	7,600 2.8%
Subcontractors	3,819 1.4%
Fleet Insurances	9,120 3.4%
Tyres	3,230 1.2%
Operators & Vehicle Licences	950 0.4%
Total Cost of Sales	105,357 39.5%
GROSS PROFIT	161,668
Gross profit margin	60.5%
OVERHEADS	
Administrative Salaries	63,540 23.8%
Insurances	19,322 7.2%
Accountancy & Audit fees	9,042 3.4%
Bank Charges	950 0.4%
Legal & Professional	7,490 2.8%
Printing & Stationery	2,075 0.8%
Telephone & Internet	3,425 1.3%
Training	4,950 1.9%
Depreciation	13,300 5.0%
Computer Expenses	2,491 0.9%
Subsistence	3,230 1.2%
Uniforms & Protective Clothing	2,533 0.9%
Advertising & Promotional Costs	10,827 4.1%
Health & Safety	1,950 0.7%
Total Overhead costs	145,125 54.3%
Overhead %age	54.3%
Total Overheads & Cost of Sales	250,482 93.8%
Net Profit	16,543 6.2%
Net profit margin	6.2%

The P&L above would seem to be perfectly functional from a review point of view. If we just wanted to see the turnover, expenses and profit for January 2021, this does the job. However, how do we know if this performance was good enough? How do we determine whether it's in line with our expectations? Above all, how do we gauge our Economic Viability in the longer term?

	Actual January		Budget January		Variance	Prior year January		Variance
PROFIT & LOSS - JANUARY 2021								
REVENUE								
Transport Income	267,025		265,000		2,025	178,223		88,802
Other Income	0		0		0	0		0
Total Revenue	267,025		265,000		2,025	178,223		88,802
COST OF SALES								
Direct Labour	27,233	10.2%	27,000	10.2%	(233)	19,066	10.7%	(8,167)
Fuel	53,405	20.0%	55,000	20.8%	1,595	38,839	21.8%	(14,566)
Fleet Maintenance	7,600	2.8%	7,500	2.8%	(100)	5,296	3.0%	(2,304)
Subcontractors	3,819	1.4%	4,000	1.5%	181	2,825	1.6%	(994)
Fleet Insurances	9,120	3.4%	9,000	3.4%	(120)	6,355	3.6%	(2,765)
Tyres	3,230	1.2%	3,500	1.3%	270	2,472	1.4%	(758)
Operators & Vehicle Licences	950	0.4%	1,000	0.4%	50	706	0.4%	(244)
Total Cost of Sales	105,357	39.5%	107,000	40.4%	1,643	75,560	42.4%	(29,797)
GROSS PROFIT	161,668		158,000		3,668	102,663		118,599
Gross profit margin	60.5%		59.6%			57.6%		133.6%
OVERHEADS								
Administrative Salaries	63,540	23.8%	63,500	24.0%	(40)	44,842	25.2%	(18,698)
Insurances	19,322	7.2%	19,750	7.5%	428	13,947	7.8%	(5,375)
Accountancy & Audit fees	9,042	3.4%	9,000	3.4%	(42)	6,355	3.6%	(2,687)
Bank Charges	950	0.4%	1,000	0.4%	50	706	0.4%	(244)
Legal & Professional	7,490	2.8%	7,500	2.8%	10	5,296	3.0%	(2,194)
Printing & Stationery	2,075	0.8%	2,000	0.8%	(75)	1,412	0.8%	(662)
Telephone & Internet	3,425	1.3%	3,500	1.3%	75	2,472	1.4%	(953)
Training	4,950	1.9%	5,000	1.9%	50	3,531	2.0%	(1,419)
Depreciation	13,300	5.0%	13,000	4.9%	(300)	9,180	5.2%	(4,120)
Computer Expenses	2,491	0.9%	2,500	0.9%	9	1,765	1.0%	(726)
Subsistence	3,230	1.2%	3,000	1.1%	(230)	2,118	1.2%	(1,112)
Uniforms & Protective Clothing	2,533	0.9%	2,500	0.9%	(33)	1,765	1.0%	(767)
Advertising & Promotional Costs	10,827	4.1%	11,000	4.2%	173	7,768	4.4%	(3,060)
Health & Safety	1,950	0.7%	2,000	0.8%	50	1,412	0.8%	(538)
Total Overhead costs	145,125	54.3%	145,250	54.8%	125	102,571	57.6%	(42,554)
Overhead %age	54.3%		54.8%			57.6%		
Total Overheads & Cost of Sales	250,482	93.8%	252,250	95.2%	1,768	178,131	99.9%	(72,351)
Net Profit	16,543	6.2%	12,750	4.8%	3,793	92	0.1%	16,451
Net profit margin	6.2%		4.8%			0.1%		

This version includes the budgeted figures. Essentially, this is what we expected to achieve in January 2021, so now we can objectively quantify whether or not this performance was good enough and whether we are still on track to achieve our budgeted performance for the year.

Variance Analysis

Variance Analysis is the key to taking control of your business. These are the individual differences between what you expected to do and what you actually did. Your ability to influence these differences will ultimately dictate your ability to succeed and whether your business is economically viable. To be clear, Variance Analysis is only concerned with the **budget** comparative, not the previous year.

Start by looking at the key figures. Revenue (aka 'Sales', or 'Turnover'), Gross Profit and Net Profit. We can see that Revenue was budgeted to be £265k, but we have actually achieved £267,025, so £2,025 up on budget. Great start.

Gross Profit (Revenue less Cost of Sales) was budgeted at £158k, but we've beaten that as well, by £3,668. Obviously this is more than the increase in budgeted revenue, so that means not only did we exceed our sales budget, we must have also reduced our costs.

Net Profit (Gross Profit less Overheads) was budgeted at £12,750, but we've smashed that by achieving £16,543, which is an improvement of £3,793. Since this is more than the increase in gross profit, we must have contained our Overheads too, so this has been a great month.

Once you've analysed the variances on these three key numbers, the next step would be to check the individual variances for any areas of concern. The format of these Management Accounts is that any adverse variances appear in red, while favourable variances are green. Realistically you should only concern yourself with significant variances, whether adverse or favourable. In the example above, all the variances are minimal, which suggests that the budget was pretty accurate and there are no real areas for concern. But let's look at some other examples.

Variance Analysis - Example 1

	Actual January		Budget January		Variance
PROFIT & LOSS - JANUARY 2021					
REVENUE					
Transport Income	373,835		265,000		108,835
Other Income	0		0		0
Total Revenue	373,835		265,000		108,835
COST OF SALES					
Direct Labour	38,126	10.2%	27,000	10.2%	(11,126)
Fuel	74,767	20.0%	55,000	20.8%	(19,767)
Fleet Maintenance	10,640	2.8%	7,500	2.8%	(3,140)
Subcontractors	5,347	1.4%	4,000	1.5%	(1,347)
Fleet Insurances	12,768	3.4%	9,000	3.4%	(3,768)
Tyres	4,522	1.2%	3,500	1.3%	(1,022)
Operators & Vehicle Licences	1,330	0.4%	1,000	0.4%	(330)
Total Cost of Sales	147,500	39.5%	107,000	40.4%	(40,500)
GROSS PROFIT	226,335		158,000		68,335
Gross profit margin	60.5%		59.6%		

In the example above, we have some huge variances. Sales is up by over 40% at £373k and Cost of Sales is up by over £40k. Look at all those red variances.

However, Gross Profit is still way more than we budgeted for, so this is great, right?

The problem is that when Revenue is so far ahead of budget, it's not immediately clear from the variances alone whether everything is still in line with expectation. This is where Proportional Analysis come into play. It's all about the percentages.

First, take a look at the Gross profit margin. This is the Gross Profit expressed as a percentage of sales. The budgeted gross margin was 59.6% and even though we were well over budget on sales revenue and costs, we're still remarkably close to the gross margin we budgeted for, at 60.5%. This is good news because it means that although costs are way higher than budgeted, they are still in line with the increase in sales.

You can tell from the expense categories that this P&L is for a transport business. So it makes sense that if revenue is so much higher than budgeted, the business must have been a lot busier than expected. If this is the case, it's reasonable to expect that the vehicles have used a lot more fuel and worn out more tyres than they would have if they had simply achieved the budgeted level of revenue. So in this case, the increase in cost of sales is in line with the increase in revenue, which is why the actual gross margin is so close to the budgeted gross margin.

However, this just means that total costs are within budget. There may be compensating variances within the individual lines that will need to be examined to avoid any nasty surprises in subsequent months.

You can see that there is a percentage to the right of each expense line, both in the actual column and the budgeted column. This percentage represents that cost as a proportion of output (Sales Revenue). So as long as these are comparable with their budgeted percentage, this confirms that each cost has only increased in line with the increase in sales and there is no cause for concern. In this example, you can see that all the percentages are quite close together, so all costs have increased in line with the increase in sales and there's nothing to worry about. We've just had a very lucrative month and no further variance analysis is required.

Variance Analysis - Example 2

	PROFIT & LOSS - JANUARY 2021		
	Actual January	Budget January	Variance
REVENUE			
Transport Income	373,835	265,000	108,835
Other Income	0	0	0
Total Revenue	373,835	265,000	108,835
COST OF SALES			
Direct Labour	12,567 3.4%	27,000 10.2%	14,433
Fuel	102,334 27.4%	55,000 20.8%	(47,334)
Fleet Maintenance	10,640 2.8%	7,500 2.8%	(3,140)
Subcontractors	5,347 1.4%	4,000 1.5%	(1,347)
Fleet Insurances	12,768 3.4%	9,000 3.4%	(3,768)
Tyres	4,522 1.2%	3,500 1.3%	(1,022)
Operators & Vehicle Licences	1,330 0.4%	1,000 0.4%	(330)
Total Cost of Sales	149,508 40.0%	107,000 40.4%	(42,508)
GROSS PROFIT	224,327	158,000	66,327
Gross profit margin	60.0%	59.6%	

In this example, Sales Revenue is, once again, up by 40%. However, there's no cause for alarm, as the gross margin is, once again, very close to the budgeted 59.6%. However, in this example we have two compensating variances on Direct labour and Fuel. Direct Labour was budgeted at 10.2% of Revenue, so we would have expected it to be around the £38k mark, but it's only £12,567, which is only 3.4% of turnover. Similarly, Fuel was expected to be only 20.8% (around £78k) but it's over £100k and 27.4%.

This would definitely need to be investigated. Either we have massively underpaid our drivers, or we have not used as many as expected, which seems odd, considering the massive upturn in sales revenue. At the same time, either we've used way more fuel than we should have, or the fuel price has gone through the roof. In both cases we need to understand what happened, because we can't reasonably expect sales to be so strong every month. If Revenue and Direct labour return to budgeted levels next month but Fuel prices remain the same, we're likely to have problems.

This is an example of how analysing variances can give you much deeper insight into the performance of your business and help you to spot and mitigate potential problems.

As alluded to earlier, Management Accounts are a diagnostic tool used to focus your analysis and make accurate decisions. They will not fix your problems for you, but they will point you in the right direction and enable you to take control of your business.

It's also important to note that both adverse and favourable variances should be analysed and investigated. If something went better than expected, it's important to understand how this happened just as it's important to understand and correct things that have gone wrong. Maximising your successes can be just as lucrative as correcting your failures.

'Bad' Management Accounts

Not all Management Accounts are created equal. The following are examples of what I have been sent when I have asked my clients to send me their Management Accounts. (Naturally, I have not used real-life snippets of my clients' data. These are fabricated examples based on documents I have been sent previously)

Hopefully, now that we have been through what Management Accounts are designed to achieve and how they work, you will be able to spot the problems with the examples below.

	Actual January	Actual February	Actual March	Actual April	Actual May	Actual June	Actual July	Actual August	Actual September	Actual October	Actual November	Actual December	Actual YTD
REVENUE													
Sales Revenue	23,313	22,782	25,389	23,259	21,092	26,274	24,728	26,100	22,821	23,656	29,327	22,197	290,938
Referral Revenue	2,582	2,344	2,769	2,888	2,029	2,766	2,019	2,161	2,321	2,437	2,447	2,531	29,294
Other Revenue	0	0	0	0	0	0	0	0	0	0	0	0	0
Total Revenue	25,895	25,126	28,158	26,147	23,121	29,040	26,747	28,261	25,142	26,093	31,774	24,728	320,232
COST OF SALES													
Subcontract	6,474	6,282	7,040	6,537	5,780	7,260	6,687	7,065	6,286	6,523	7,944	6,182	80,058
Direct labour	9,063	8,794	9,855	9,151	8,092	10,164	9,361	9,891	8,800	9,133	11,121	8,655	112,081
Other direct expenses	0	0	0	0	0	0	0	0	0	0	0	0	0
Total Cost of Sales	15,537	15,076	16,895	15,688	13,873	17,424	16,048	16,957	15,085	15,656	19,064	14,837	192,139
GROSS PROFIT	10,358	10,050	11,263	10,459	9,248	11,616	10,699	11,304	10,057	10,437	12,710	9,891	128,093
Gross profit margin	40.0%	40.0%	40.0%	40.0%	40.0%	40.0%	40.0%	40.0%	40.0%	40.0%	40.0%	40.0%	40.0%
OVERHEADS													
Advertising & Marketing	3,884	3,769	4,224	3,922	3,468	4,356	4,012	4,239	3,771	3,914	4,766	3,709	48,035
Professional fees	0	0	0	0	0	0	0	0	0	0	0	0	0
General Expenses	518	503	563	523	462	581	535	565	503	522	635	495	6,405
Legal Expenses	209	214	201	254	220	249	232	200	228	200	229	217	2,653
Insurance	350	350	350	350	350	350	350	350	350	350	350	350	4,200
IT Software and Consumables	234	248	222	253	282	232	281	231	251	263	229	203	2,929
Repairs & Maintenance	275	266	242	296	278	267	260	282	242	223	289	214	3,134
Directors' Remuneration	2,870	2,618	2,031	2,016	2,762	2,239	2,630	2,725	2,686	2,101	2,855	2,125	29,658
Training	261	281	277	277	286	233	298	215	291	241	213	216	3,089
Telephone & Internet	291	218	213	262	215	270	228	240	266	294	240	204	2,941
Depreciation expense	271	218	256	249	259	208	297	249	268	261	214	201	2,951
Total Overhead costs	9,163	8,684	8,579	8,402	8,583	8,985	9,123	9,296	8,856	8,369	10,021	7,934	105,994
Overhead %age	35.4%	34.6%	30.5%	32.1%	37.1%	30.9%	34.1%	32.9%	35.2%	32.1%	31.5%	32.1%	33.1%
Total Overheads & Cost of Sales	24,700	23,760	25,474	24,090	22,455	26,409	25,171	26,253	23,941	24,025	29,085	22,771	298,134
Net Profit	1,195	1,366	2,684	2,057	666	2,631	1,576	2,008	1,201	2,068	2,689	1,957	22,098
Net profit margin	4.6%	5.4%	9.5%	7.9%	2.9%	9.1%	5.9%	7.1%	4.8%	7.9%	8.5%	7.9%	6.9%

The above example is just a list of P&Ls for each month of the year. This is an excellent functional document and should certainly be part of your board pack for review, but in isolation this doesn't even come close to achieving the functionality of a set of Management Accounts. No comparatives, no Balance Sheet, no variances.

	Actual January		Budget January		Variance	Prior year January		Variance
REVENUE								
Sales Revenue	38,962		38,000		962	28,500		10,462
Referral Revenue	42,554		42,000		554	31,500		11,054
Other Revenue	0		0		0	0		0
Total Revenue	81,516		80,000		1,516	60,000		21,516
COST OF SALES								
Subcontract	734	0.9%	0	0.0%	(734)	0	0.0%	(734)
Direct labour - van driver	4,626	5.7%	4,000	5.0%	(626)	3,000	5.0%	(1,626)
Direct labour - fitters	4,835	5.9%	4,000	5.0%	(835)	3,000	5.0%	(1,835)
Direct labour - workstation A	1,232	1.5%	1,000	1.3%	(232)	750	1.3%	(482)
Direct labour - workstation B	4,055	5.0%	4,000	5.0%	(55)	3,000	5.0%	(1,055)
Direct labour - workstation C	4,502	5.5%	4,000	5.0%	(502)	3,000	5.0%	(1,502)
Direct labour - workstation D	1,738	2.1%	1,000	1.3%	(738)	750	1.3%	(988)
Direct labour - workstation E	3,933	4.8%	3,000	3.8%	(933)	2,250	3.8%	(1,683)
Packaging - boxes	4,347	5.3%	4,000	5.0%	(347)	3,000	5.0%	(1,347)
Packaging - tape	1,292	1.6%	1,000	1.3%	(292)	750	1.3%	(542)
Packaging - bubble wrap	940	1.2%	0	0.0%	(940)	0	0.0%	(940)
Packaging - banding	1,609	2.0%	1,000	1.3%	(609)	750	1.3%	(859)
Other direct expenses	2,617	3.2%	2,000	2.5%	(617)	1,500	2.5%	(1,117)
Total Cost of Sales	36,480	44.8%	29,000	36.3%	(7,480)	21,750	36.3%	(14,730)
GROSS PROFIT	45,036		51,000		(5,964)	38,250		6,786
Gross profit margin	55.2%		63.8%			63.8%		31.5%
OVERHEADS								
Advertising & Marketing	438	0.5%	400	0.5%	(38)	300	0.5%	(138)
Professional fees	484	0.6%	400	0.5%	(84)	300	0.5%	(184)
General Expenses	304	0.4%	300	0.4%	(4)	225	0.4%	(79)
Legal Expenses	327	0.4%	300	0.4%	(27)	225	0.4%	(102)
Pest control	211	0.3%	200	0.3%	(11)	150	0.3%	(61)
Rent	247	0.3%	200	0.3%	(47)	150	0.3%	(97)
Rates	240	0.3%	200	0.3%	(40)	150	0.3%	(90)
Water	415	0.5%	400	0.5%	(15)	300	0.5%	(115)
Gas	382	0.5%	300	0.4%	(82)	225	0.4%	(157)
Electricity	255	0.3%	200	0.3%	(55)	150	0.3%	(105)
TV Licence	318	0.4%	300	0.4%	(18)	225	0.4%	(93)
Car insurance	337	0.4%	300	0.4%	(37)	225	0.4%	(112)
Van insurance	490	0.6%	400	0.5%	(90)	300	0.5%	(190)
Public liability insurance	395	0.5%	300	0.4%	(95)	225	0.4%	(170)
Employers liability insurance	292	0.4%	200	0.3%	(92)	150	0.3%	(142)
HR costs - Training	1,902	2.3%	1,900	2.4%	(2)	1,425	2.4%	(477)
HR costs - Culture	633	0.8%	600	0.8%	(33)	450	0.8%	(183)
HR costs - Employee welfare	952	1.2%	900	1.1%	(52)	675	1.1%	(277)
HR costs - Benefits	1,883	2.3%	1,800	2.3%	(83)	1,350	2.3%	(533)
Telephone	498	0.6%	400	0.5%	(98)	300	0.5%	(198)
Mobile phone	1,700	2.1%	1,700	2.1%	0	1,275	2.1%	(425)
Broadband	1,204	1.5%	1,200	1.5%	(4)	900	1.5%	(304)
Printing costs	1,741	2.1%	1,700	2.1%	(41)	1,275	2.1%	(466)
Stationery	1,990	2.4%	1,900	2.4%	(90)	1,425	2.4%	(565)
Postage	1,948	2.4%	1,900	2.4%	(48)	1,425	2.4%	(523)
Courier costs	1,883	2.3%	1,800	2.3%	(83)	1,350	2.3%	(533)
IT support	1,846	2.3%	1,800	2.3%	(46)	1,350	2.3%	(496)
IT services	351	0.4%	300	0.4%	(51)	225	0.4%	(126)
Software	1,853	2.3%	1,800	2.3%	(53)	1,350	2.3%	(503)
Bad debt provision	458	0.6%	400	0.5%	(58)	300	0.5%	(158)
Rates consultant	1,057	1.3%	1,000	1.3%	(57)	750	1.3%	(307)
Financial consultant	1,191	1.5%	1,100	1.4%	(91)	825	1.4%	(366)
Branding consultant	556	0.7%	500	0.6%	(56)	375	0.6%	(181)
Motor vehicles - Fuel	689	0.8%	600	0.8%	(89)	450	0.8%	(239)
Motor vehicles - Parking	790	1.0%	700	0.9%	(90)	525	0.9%	(265)
Motor vehicles - Cleaning	1,219	1.5%	1,200	1.5%	(19)	900	1.5%	(319)
Motor vehicles - Fines	1,028	1.3%	1,000	1.3%	(28)	750	1.3%	(278)
Motor vehicles - Tolls	1,952	2.4%	1,900	2.4%	(52)	1,425	2.4%	(527)
Depreciation Plant & Machinery	429	0.5%	400	0.5%	(29)	300	0.5%	(129)
Depreciation Computers	610	0.7%	600	0.8%	(10)	450	0.8%	(160)
Depreciation Fixtures & Fittings	1,773	2.2%	1,700	2.1%	(73)	1,275	2.1%	(498)
Depreciation Land & Buildings	263	0.3%	200	0.3%	(63)	150	0.3%	(113)
Depreciation Leasehold Imp	536	0.7%	500	0.6%	(36)	375	0.6%	(161)
Cleaning - offices	345	0.4%	300	0.4%	(45)	225	0.4%	(120)
Cleaning - yard	1,371	1.7%	1,300	1.6%	(71)	975	1.6%	(396)
Cleaning - factory	1,776	2.2%	1,700	2.1%	(76)	1,275	2.1%	(501)
Cleaning - car park	1,667	2.0%	1,600	2.0%	(67)	1,200	2.0%	(467)
Security costs	819	1.0%	800	1.0%	(19)	600	1.0%	(219)
Fire alarm costs	903	1.1%	900	1.1%	(3)	675	1.1%	(228)
Intruder alarm costs	717	0.9%	700	0.9%	(17)	525	0.9%	(192)
Waste disposal	229	0.3%	200	0.3%	(29)	150	0.3%	(79)
Skip hire	586	0.7%	500	0.6%	(86)	375	0.6%	(211)
Repairs & Maintenance	1,698	2.1%	1,600	2.0%	(98)	1,200	2.0%	(498)
Yard repairs	1,047	1.3%	1,000	1.3%	(47)	750	1.3%	(297)
Building repairs	468	0.6%	400	0.5%	(68)	300	0.5%	(168)
Office maintenance costs	928	1.1%	900	1.1%	(28)	675	1.1%	(253)
Total Overhead costs	50,624	62.1%	47,800	59.8%	(2,824)	35,850	59.8%	(14,774)
Overhead %age	62.1%		59.8%			59.8%		
Total Overheads & Cost of Sales	87,104	106.9%	76,800	96.0%	(10,304)	57,600	96.0%	(29,504)
Net Profit	-5,588	-6.9%	3,200	4.0%	(8,788)	2,400	4.0%	(7,988)
Net profit margin	-6.9%		4.0%			4.0%		

The P&L on the previous page is far too 'busy'. Management Accounts are supposed to be a functional report, giving you an overview of your performance. To produce something this detailed would be pointless and would take too long to review and analyse. Remember that they are supposed to be a diagnostic tool that points you in the right direction, not something that analyses every single account in your accounting system.

As a side note, to create a budget this detailed would also be a futile exercise. It would take months to produce and would almost certainly be inaccurate

	Actual January		Budget January		Variance	Prior year January		Variance
REVENUE	81,516		80,000		1,516	60,000		21,516
COST OF SALES	36,480	44.8%	29,000	36.3%	(7,480)	21,750	36.3%	(14,730)
GROSS PROFIT	45,036		51,000		(5,964)	38,250		6,786
Gross profit margin	55.2%		63.8%			63.8%		31.5%
OVERHEADS	50,624	62.1%	47,800	59.8%	(2,824)	35,850	59.8%	(14,774)
Overhead %age	62.1%		59.8%			59.8%		
Total Overheads & Cost of Sales	87,104	106.9%	76,800	96.0%	(10,304)	57,600	96.0%	(29,504)
Net Profit	-5,588	-6.9%	3,200	4.0%	(8,788)	2,400	4.0%	(7,988)
Net profit margin	-6.9%		4.0%			4.0%		

This is the opposite of the previous example. Nowhere near enough detail to be able to review variances accurately and identify areas of concern. The figures would still be reliable, but they don't give you enough data to make decisions or evaluate the performance of the business.

Summary

So there you have it. Flawless Performance Evaluation, which covers off the first and most important part of the Control Cycle.

So now that we know how we're doing, let's see whether it's good enough.

Chapter 8 - Economic Viability

What is Economic Viability?

Economic Viability in this context means the degree to which the business is viable in both the current economic climate and the reasonably predictable future economic climate.

In simpler terms, it means 'does the business work'.

Let's say you started a business selling a specific product, which you could source in China for US$20 and sell in the UK for £25. At the time of placing your first order with the supplier, the exchange rate was 1.4 US$ to 1GB£. This meant that your purchase cost was actually £14.29, leaving you a profit of £10.71.

However, the $20 purchase price doesn't include shipping, selling fees or other costs, so calculating your actual profit per unit would look something like this:

GBP unit cost ($20/1.4)	14.29
Shipping cost (per unit)	1.20
VAT/duty	4.00
Listing fee	1.61
P&P	3.90
Total cost	25.00
Selling price	25.00
Profit	0.00
Margin	0.0%

As you can see, the business makes no profit once all costs are factored in, so this is not a viable business in its current form.

So let's say you manage to find a cheaper supplier and reduce the purchase cost to $15. This also reduces the VAT and excise duty, which are based on the purchase price. You also find a cheaper packaging supplier and reduce the P&P cost for sending the product to your customers. With these reductions factored in, your profit improves as follows:

GBP unit cost ($15/1.4)	10.71
Shipping cost (per unit)	1.20
VAT/duty	3.00
Listing fee	1.61
P&P	3.50
Total cost	20.02
Selling price	25.00
Profit	4.98
Margin	20%

Now that you're making almost £5 profit on each item sold, which is a 20% margin, the business could be considered viable, at least in the current economic conditions.

But conditions change, and your margin is subject to those changes.

Following a presidential election in the US the USD/GBP exchange rate drops to 1.20, which has a significant impact on your purchase costs. At the same time, a global oil shortage means an increase in shipping costs, which also takes a bite out of your profit.

GBP unit cost ($15/1.4)	12.50
Shipping cost (per unit)	3.00
VAT/duty	3.00
Listing fee	1.61
P&P	3.50
Total cost	23.61
Selling price	25.00
Profit	1.39
Margin	6%

Suddenly, despite buying and selling at the same prices, your margins are reduced by 70%.

'eBay Economics'

These three examples raise several noteworthy points. Firstly, they illustrate the importance of Performance Evaluation and why it must be carried out before assessing your Economic Viability. I've met business owners who have no idea of their true margins because they don't monitor or calculate the actual revenues and costs they are working with. I refer to this as 'eBay economics' because I've heard many people talk about how you can buy x from China for £x and sell it on eBay for £x and 'make a killing'. These are the same people who simply deduct the £14.29 purchase cost from the £25 selling price and can't understand why they're not making any money.

Ultimately, without carrying out performance evaluation to understand the true margins of your operation, you can't possibly assess your economic viability and therefore ascertain whether you have a sustainable business or not.

Of course these are simple examples, used to illustrate a point, but I have worked with multi-million pound clients who are convinced (based on instinct and not much else) that they're making a 40% margin and can't understand why they don't have any money in the bank. Once we devise and implement monthly reporting, they are stunned to discover that their actual gross margin is more like 17%. This often comes as a shock, but actually it's the beginning of a process that will enable them to achieve much better results. Knowing the truth is always more constructive than working with historical delusions, unfounded estimates or 'gut feel'.

Adapt to Survive

Another point illustrated by the second example above is the importance of entrepreneurship in business. Although the business didn't work in the first example, finding new suppliers to reduce costs improved the margin and turned it into an economically viable operation. Of course there will be limits to this and it's important to avoid 'flogging a dead horse', but pushing boundaries is a key attribute of a successful entrepreneur and business leader. The key to this is to know what you need to achieve. This is where Breakeven Analysis comes in.

Of course, your goal in business is not to break even, it's to make a profit. But you also need to know the lines you can't afford to cross in the pursuit of that profit. Your breakeven point is not intended to be a goal, it's intended to give you a baseline for planning. In the case of the second example above, you're making a 20% margin. I've said above that this makes it a viable operation, but this is a subjective point. If this business is intended to replace your 9-5 job, then maybe you need at least a 30% margin in order to pay your bills. On this basis, the business is not viable, even after improving your margin by finding new suppliers. You can try to reduce costs further, but if this proves impossible, you will need to find something else to do for a living.

Sustaining Your Viability

The third example takes a viable business and makes it non-viable. This shows that even after you've worked hard to reduce costs and improve your margin, forces beyond your control can undo that hard work. Again, it would depend on your benchmark of 'viability' but a 6% margin would generally be considered unworkable.

Another key point raised in the third example is the lack of control you have over external factors. The only real control you have in a scenario like this is your reaction to the changes in exchange rate and shipping costs. The 'Braking Distance' principle dictates that you, as a business owner/director, should be actively monitoring the external factors your business is most sensitive to. This means you would be aware of any likely fluctuations in those metrics and have countermeasures in place, such as a currency hedging strategy, or contractual pricing with shipping companies. We will examine this in more detail later in the book, but the principle of accountability means that you should have your finger on the pulse when it comes to factors outside of your control.

Budgeting - Setting the Benchmark

Ultimately, assessing the economic viability of your business comes down to setting a benchmark in advance, then reviewing your performance against it every month. If you consistently achieve the goal you've set for yourself, your business is viable. If not, it isn't. It's really that simple. This benchmark is set when you create your budget for the year.

As mentioned in the previous chapter, budgeting is absolutely vital for Performance Evaluation, Economic Viability and for Financial Control in general. Essentially, your budget should outline what you expect to achieve over a 12-month period in terms of revenue, costs and profit. It should be neither best case nor worst case, it should be 'most-likely' case. It should be the most likely result based on the resources you control at the beginning of the year and any resources you can secure during the year (as long as the cost of securing those resources is also included in the budget).

A budget is not a target, although it is often the basis of targets. For example a sales rep may be incentivised to 'beat budget' by 25% and rewarded with a bonus if they achieve this. The fact that it represents the most likely outcome means bonuses should not be earned by achieving it.

If the budget is well-thought out, the economic environment is fully understood and all estimates are accurate, your budget should be achievable and therefore your benchmark for Economic Viability is set. The first year budget will often be the basis of a 3-year or 5-year plan, and these plans should be updated based on the performance against the first year's budget.

Three Questions

Once the budget has been put in place and each month has its own specific budget, which takes account of seasonality during the year, you are in a position to carry out monthly Performance Evaluation and use this to gauge your Economic Viability. In short, you're in a position to cover off two of the three Elements of Control in the Control Cycle.

Once you have achieved this, you should aim to answer the following three questions at the end of each month.

1. How are we doing?
2. Is it good enough?
3. Is it sustainable?

The answers to these questions are not a matter of opinion and should be answered in absolute terms.

"How are we doing?" - This is now a mathematical question. You have Management Accounts to tell you **what** you've achieved and a budget to dictate what you **should have** achieved. Whatever the result, you can express it as a percentage of your budget. You can also pinpoint the exact areas you have fallen short, or excelled, or simply achieved what you thought you would. As you progress through the year, it's important to monitor the cumulative performance against your budget, not just each month in isolation. This is how you really find out how you're doing.

"Is it good enough?" - Again, this is now a simple matter of looking at your Management Accounts and identifying whether your economic performance is good enough. Even if you've fallen short of your budgeted performance, the result may be 'good enough' to sustain the business in the short term. This isn't a matter of opinion. It's determined by the degree to which the business has 'beaten' its breakeven point.

"Is it sustainable?" - After reviewing the external sensitivities of your business (eg exchange rates, material prices, market factors) and the direction they are going in, while also tracking your performance against your own budget, you will be able to determine whether the business is likely to be able to sustain its viability in the medium/long-term. Again, this isn't down to interpretation. Using quarterly forecasting, you will be able to ascertain the trajectory of the business and whether it will achieve the profits required to mitigate the impact of likely external forces.

Hopefully you are now beginning to understand how control is manifested and maintained and the massive benefits these processes will bring to your business. Without performance evaluation, you don't know how you're doing. With unreliable performance evaluation, you have a distorted view of how you're doing. With Management Accounts you know exactly how you're doing and how you should be doing.

Breakeven Analysis

So how do we determine our Breakeven point. First you need to establish the Gross Profit you need to achieve in order to pay for your overheads. This is calculated from the Management Accounts. Let's review the P&L we looked at in the previous chapter.

	PROFIT & LOSS - JANUARY 2021					
	Actual January		Budget January		Variance	Prior year January		Variance

	Actual January		Budget January		Variance	Prior year January		Variance
REVENUE								
Transport Income	267,025		265,000		2,025	178,223		88,802
Other Income	0		0		0	0		0
Total Revenue	267,025		265,000		2,025	178,223		88,802
COST OF SALES								
Direct Labour	27,233	10.2%	27,000	10.2%	(233)	19,066	10.7%	(8,167)
Fuel	53,405	20.0%	55,000	20.8%	1,595	38,839	21.8%	(14,566)
Fleet Maintenance	7,600	2.8%	7,500	2.8%	(100)	5,296	3.0%	(2,304)
Subcontractors	3,819	1.4%	4,000	1.5%	181	2,825	1.6%	(994)
Fleet Insurances	9,120	3.4%	9,000	3.4%	(120)	6,355	3.6%	(2,765)
Tyres	3,230	1.2%	3,500	1.3%	270	2,472	1.4%	(758)
Operators & Vehicle Licences	950	0.4%	1,000	0.4%	50	706	0.4%	(244)
Total Cost of Sales	105,357	39.5%	107,000	40.4%	1,643	75,560	42.4%	(29,797)
GROSS PROFIT	161,668		158,000		3,668	102,663		118,599
Gross profit margin	60.5%		59.6%			57.6%		133.6%
OVERHEADS								
Administrative Salaries	63,540	23.8%	63,500	24.0%	(40)	44,842	25.2%	(18,698)
Insurances	19,322	7.2%	19,750	7.5%	428	13,947	7.8%	(5,375)
Accountancy & Audit fees	9,042	3.4%	9,000	3.4%	(42)	6,355	3.6%	(2,687)
Bank Charges	950	0.4%	1,000	0.4%	50	706	0.4%	(244)
Legal & Professional	7,490	2.8%	7,500	2.8%	10	5,296	3.0%	(2,194)
Printing & Stationery	2,075	0.8%	2,000	0.8%	(75)	1,412	0.8%	(662)
Telephone & Internet	3,425	1.3%	3,500	1.3%	75	2,472	1.4%	(953)
Training	4,950	1.9%	5,000	1.9%	50	3,531	2.0%	(1,419)
Depreciation	13,300	5.0%	13,000	4.9%	(300)	9,180	5.2%	(4,120)
Computer Expenses	2,491	0.9%	2,500	0.9%	9	1,765	1.0%	(726)
Subsistence	3,230	1.2%	3,000	1.1%	(230)	2,118	1.2%	(1,112)
Uniforms & Protective Clothing	2,533	0.9%	2,500	0.9%	(33)	1,765	1.0%	(767)
Advertising & Promotional Costs	10,827	4.1%	11,000	4.2%	173	7,768	4.4%	(3,060)
Health & Safety	1,950	0.7%	2,000	0.8%	50	1,412	0.8%	(538)
Total Overhead costs	145,125	54.3%	145,250	54.8%	125	102,571	57.6%	(42,554)
Overhead %age	54.3%		54.8%			57.6%		
Total Overheads & Cost of Sales	250,482	93.8%	252,250	95.2%	1,768	178,131	99.9%	(72,351)
Net Profit	16,543	6.2%	12,750	4.8%	3,793	92	0.1%	16,451
Net profit margin	6.2%		4.8%			0.1%		

So the total overhead costs in the month were £145,125, so this is the amount of gross profit we need to generate in order to break even.

Breakeven Profit is therefore £145,125

We know that the gross margin achieved in the month was 60.5%, as shown in the Management Accounts above. To calculate the Breakeven Sales for the month, we simply divide the Breakeven Profit by the Gross Margin.

145,125 / 60.5% = 239,876

So the Breakeven Sales Revenue (ie sales revenue required to break even), in this month only, is £239,876. The actual sales achieved in the month is £267,025, so we were well ahead of the Breakeven Point.

This is obviously after the month has ended, but if you wanted to know the budgeted Breakeven Point before the month started (to set a target for your sales team, for example), just do the same calculation using the budgeted figures.

Budgeted Total Overhead Costs = £145,250 (aka Breakeven Profit)
Budgeted Gross Margin = 59.6%
145,250 / 59.6% = 243,708

So the budgeted Breakeven Point was sales revenue of £243,708. The fact that this is higher than the actual Breakeven Point shows that we have achieved a better result than budgeted (which we can see anyway from the Management Accounts).

Margin of Safety

The difference between the Breakeven Point and the budgeted sales revenue is known as the 'Margin of Safety'. This represents the amount of sales you could afford to forego before you start to lose money. The margin of safety is calculated as follows:

Margin of Safety = Budgeted Sales - Budgeted Breakeven Point

So in the case of this example:
Margin of Safety = 265,000 - 243,708 = £21,292

This means that sales revenue could have been reduced by £21,292 before the company made a loss.

The Margin of Safety can also be expressed as a percentage. For example the sales revenue could have dropped by 8.03% (21,292 / 265,000).

There are several reasons this information may be useful. If you know you can reduce revenue and still make profit, this gives you the opportunity to run promotions. It also helps with decision-making when going through temporary downturns, such as a recession.

Breakeven Analysis is a complex subject and a deep understanding of it can help you to fine tune your strategy. Understanding exactly which product, customer, site or department is generating different levels of profit gives you another level of control over your business.

Diagnosis and Investigation

It has to be said that, for all their flawless reliability, Management Accounts do not actually solve problems in their own right. They are a diagnostic tool that directs you to a problem but fixing that problem is another matter. This is where supporting reports should be included in your Management Accounts pack. Naturally these supporting reports will be specific to a business so it's hard for me to specify which reports should be included. Ultimately though, they need to correlate (or at least reconcile) to the Management Accounts.

For example, if you have fallen well short of your budgeted sales revenue, you should be able to run a report showing a breakdown of your sales figures for the month. But if the Management Accounts show sales revenue of £64,000 and your sales report shows £72,000, then either the sales report is wrong, or some of your sales have been prepaid/accrued into a different period. You need to understand this difference before you investigate any further.

Once this difference has been ironed out, deeper analysis can be carried out to understand why sales were so much lower than budgeted. It's also important to analyse good results, as these are often overlooked. Understanding the reason you've done well is just as important as knowing why you've fallen short.

Sustaining Your Economic Viability

The key to sustaining your viability is the Braking Distance Principle, which I will keep referring back to as it's a key element of accountability in business.

Once you've established a business that 'works' as per your Management Accounts and budget, you need to make sure nothing else derails it, as in the third example at the start of this chapter, where all the good work was undone by currency exchange rates and increases in shipping costs. Ultimately, all business are vulnerable to changes in external factors they can't control, and the only way to combat this is readiness. Chapter 15 of this book goes into a lot more detail on this, but it's vitally important to accept and embrace the accountability associated with running a business.

There are all manner of external factors your business may have to contend with, depending on your sector, industry, location and several other variables. However, the following apply to all business, so these are a useful starting point:

1. Market - The market in which the organisation operates
2. Behaviours - Customer behaviours and the forces which impact them
3. External regulation - HMRC, legislation, affiliation, accreditation
4. External events - Recession, terrorism, pandemics, natural disasters

Only extremely large companies can hope to influence any of these factors, and this book is not aimed at the people running those companies, so in most cases, you will have no control over them, only your reaction to them. The best way to give yourself more time to react is to remember the Braking Distance Principle. Keep your ear to the ground, review your sensitivities and scan the horizon for potential problems. That's how to ensure long-term Economic Viability.

Remember that the best strategic position is always "How are we insufficient and what can we do to rectify that?".

Chapter 9 - Compliance

Compliance

As outlined previously, Compliance relates to the fulfilment of external obligations, whether mandatory or voluntary.

As you will see during this chapter, compliance is a very broad concept, as all business have different circumstances, different responsibilities and different obligations. For me to attempt to outline all of them in this book would be futile, not to mention impossible. Instead, I will focus on concepts and techniques which can be adapted to fit any business.

External Obligations

So what do we mean by external obligations? Here are some well-known examples:

- HMRC deadlines (VAT returns, Corporation Tax, PAYE)
- Pension contributions
- GDPR and data protection
- Health & Safety obligations
- Legislation in general

When music retail giant HMV appointed administrators in 2013, they were £110m in debt. Almost 20% of this debt was owed to HMRC. This is a powerful illustration of how neglecting your external obligations can exacerbate problems.

The reason the examples above are well-known is because all businesses need to comply with them. However, there are a whole raft of not-so-well-known examples, which apply to some but not all businesses.

- **The Apprentice Levy** - All businesses with a wage bill above a certain threshold must contribute a percentage to the apprentice levy
- **PRS/PPL** - If you play music in the workplace which is audible to more than one person, you need a licence to do so. Many businesses are unaware of this restriction.
- **ISO** - Any business certified to an ISO standard must pass audits to

retain their certification and failure to do so may lead to the loss of key customers and ultimately business failure.

- **Corporate and Social Responsibilities** - These are often self-imposed social obligations, such as tree-planting or charitable initiatives. However, if they are publicised and then not carried out, the PR backlash can be damaging to a business.

The examples above represent a small number of obligations faced by many businesses but there are countless others, all of which need to be managed carefully to ensure smooth running of a business.

Neglecting Your Obligations

Most of the examples listed above are administered by well-known agencies, but there are even more obscure examples which can dramatically undermine your business if neglected.

A former client of mine was an e-commerce seller, selling on multiple platforms. The largest of these platforms was Amazon, who impose stringent conditions on their sellers to ensure their customers receive a quality service. If your customer service drops below a certain level, Amazon are entitled to withhold your payments until your performance improves.

The business in question was vaguely aware of this restriction, but didn't bother to monitor their seller performance or consider what would happen if they breached the threshold required by Amazon. Inevitably, they fell foul of the system and payments were stopped. This meant that they had virtually no cash coming in and were unable to pay their suppliers on time. Since the business was already struggling, they had a history of paying late and several suppliers saw this as the last straw, putting their account on hold. This in turn meant that they were unable to order the stock they needed to fulfil Amazon orders and improve their seller status. The business was forced to take out a loan to pay off the suppliers and eventually the cash from Amazon began to flow again, but the loan repayments added to the cash flow concerns and eventually the business failed.

This is a tragic tale but it's also a good example of how neglecting your external obligations can disrupt even the most profitable of businesses.

External Events

The obligations we've looked at so far consist mainly of enforcement or impositions on the business by external agencies or third parties. Another factor, which is much harder to anticipate and manage, is the effect of external events on the business. Technically these could be described as influences or forces more than obligations but nevertheless, as a business owner, you have an obligation to mitigate the impact of external events to whatever extent is possible.

Accountability

This word appears many times throughout this book because I have learned over the years that Accountability and Consistency are key attributes required to succeed in business.

This applies to Compliance at least as much as it does to the other two Elements of Control, perhaps even more so. When establishing your Performance Evaluation and Economic Viability, you will at least have known figures and values to work with. By contrast, Compliance relies much more heavily on your ability to go looking for the unknown and then figure out how to control it, or at least mitigate the impact of it.

Nevertheless, the acceptance of your own accountability is still a vital factor. Ignorance is no defence and HMRC won't let you off just because you were unaware of an obligation. Penalties and restrictions can be imposed if regulations are breached and suddenly all your performance evaluation and economic viability can be lost.

Your accountability also includes the obligation to constantly 'scan the horizon' for external events which could impact the business and establish a plan to deal with them.

Remember the braking distance principle, if you look far enough ahead and always leave time to think, you give yourself the resilience to handle almost anything.

Chapter 10 - The Transaction Flow

The Transaction Flow

Remember in Chapter 6, when we looked at accounting concepts? The first of these was the Accounting Equation.

Equity = (Assets - Liabilities)

The reason this equation holds true is that every transaction in your business is recorded in one of the categories referred to in the equation: Asset, Liability or Equity.

To break this down a little further, we need to introduce some detail around the word 'Equity'. In Chapter 6, we said that this Equity consists of capital (put in by the owner of the business) and any profit earned and retained by the business since it began trading. To expand on that concept, let's look at the components of that profit.

Profit, essentially, is simply income minus expenses. So if we were to restate the Accounting Equation in a more detailed way, it would look like this:

(Capital + (Income - Expenses)) = (Assets - Liabilities)

These are the five categories that every transaction in your business will ultimately fall into, and this is why the Accounting Equation (and Double Entry Accounting) works.

Every transaction in your business will impact at least two of these categories (hence the term 'Double entry'), keeping the equation balanced.

- **Cash sale of product** - Increase **Income** (Sales account) and increase **Asset** (Bank account)
    - This transaction increases profit on the left hand side of the equation and increases an asset on the right hand side, so the equation still balances.

- **Repayment of loan** - Reduce **Liability** (Loan account) and reduce **Asset** (Bank account)
    - This transaction reduces both a liability and an asset, which is a neutral movement on the right hand side of the equation, so the equation still balances.

- **Stock purchase on credit** - Increase **Asset** (Stock account) and increase **Liability** (Supplier credit account)
  - This transaction increases an asset and increases a liability, which is a neutral movement on the right hand side of the equation, so the equation still balances.

- **Pay mobile phone bill by direct debit** - Increase **Expense** (Mobile phone account) and reduce **Asset** (Bank account)
  - This transaction increases expenses (therefore reducing profit) on the left hand side of the equation, and reduces an asset on the right hand side, so the equation still balances.

Some transactions will reduce and increase accounts within the same category, for example a stock purchase paid for in cash - Increase **Asset** (Stock Account) and reduce **Asset** (Bank Account).

There are no exceptions to this rule. Every transaction reduces one and increases another, hence the double entry impact. This ultimately leads to the flawless reliability we saw in Chapter 7.

NB: There are no examples here for Capital transactions, since they are rare, unless the business is traded on the stock exchange.

An easy way to remember these categories is with the mnemonic 'ALICE'

- Asset
- Liability
- Income
- Capital
- Expense

Although all transactions will eventually drop down into profit, they will usually transition between the five categories listed above until they get there. The transaction flow is the passage a transaction takes through your business, moving between the 'ALICE' categories until they crystallise within your retained profit.

So let's look at the Transaction Flow and how it relates to these categories.
There are four distinct stages within the Transaction Flow.

Income and **Expenses** are captured as they enter the business

If these transactions are invoiced and paid in the same period (eg in retail cash transactions), they are recognised as **Profit** in the period.

If there is a timing difference (ie an invoice is received in one period but payable/receivable in a later period), the transactions are recorded as either an **Asset** or **Liability**, depending on whether they are owed to or by the business.

Once the transactions have been captured and balanced, the Management Accounts can be created and the results analysed using a robust reporting framework.

After reports have been reviewed and analysed, the resulting data is used to evaluate the financial position of the business in the context of the economic environment.

As you can see from this diagram, the first two stages of the transaction flow lead to the creation of the Management Accounts, which then enables the analysis and economic evaluation of the business. This means that the first two stages will satisfy the Accounting Equation by defining the Assets, Liabilities, Income and Expenses as at the end of the period being reported on.

Timing Differences in Recognition and Settlement

It's important to understand the significance of timing differences in accounting for financial transactions. If a supplier invoice for £100 is received and paid in the same period, it's recorded as an **Expense** and the reduction of an **Asset** (the bank balance).

However, if the same invoice is received in one period but paid in a later period, it's still recognised as an **Expense** in the period but a **Liability** if it remains unpaid at the end of the period (because it's still owed to the supplier). Without doing this, the Accounting Equation would fail, as profit (equity) would be reduced, but there would be no counteracting entry in the accounts. Failing to recognise this liability would give a misleading view of the financial position of the business. This would be similar to relying on today's bank balance when you know you have multiple direct debits due out tomorrow.

Regardless of any timing differences, the **Expense** is included in the **Profit** calculation for the period, so to keep the Accounting Equation balanced, the entries would be as follows:

Example 1 - £100 Invoice received and paid in the same period:
Profit (equity) reduces by £100
Assets (bank balance) reduce by £100
Equity will still balance to (Assets - Liabilities) and therefore the Accounting Equation balances

Example 2 - £100 Invoice received in one period and paid in a later period:
Profit (equity) reduces by £100
Liabilities (purchase ledger) increase by £100
Equity will still balance to (Assets - Liabilities) and therefore the Accounting Equation balances

The same is equally true if we replace the supplier invoice with a sales invoice. If a sales invoice for £100 is paid in the same period it's issued, **Profit** increases by £100 while **Assets** (bank balance) will also increase by £100. If this invoice is paid in a later period, again, **Profit** increases by £100 while

Assets (sales ledger) also increases by £100. Again, both sides of the Accounting Equation increase by £100, so the equation balances.

This is what we mean by 'balancing', which is the second stage of the Transaction Flow.

The Four Points of Control

The Transaction Flow is the basis of The Four Points of Control, which is the method used to prove the numbers in the P&L, to arrive at the profit figure for the period. This concept is explored in the next chapter.

Chapter 11 - Four Points of Control

The Four Points of Control

The Four Points of Control framework represents the four stages of the Transaction Flow. This is the fundamental process by which control is achieved.

If the Three Elements of Control are WHAT you need to achieve in business, the Four Points of Control are HOW you achieve it. This is the framework which fundamentally ensures that all transactions are captured, balanced, analysed and then used to evaluate your position in the economic environment.

The Four Points of Control are:

- Cash & Ledgers
- Assets & Liabilities

- Reporting
- External Factors

As you can see, the first letter of each spells out the mnemonic 'CARE'. This is entirely coincidental and not by design, but there's no denying it's a handy way to remember them all in order. The order is important, since each point of control corresponds to a stage of the Transaction Flow. In fact, a more accurate visual representation of the four points would be as follows:

The reason for this depiction is that the first two points of control are focused on **achieving** Performance Evaluation, while points three and four are **driven by** your Performance Evaluation. In other words, points one and two lead to the creation of Management Accounts, whereas the third and fourth points use the data generated by the Management Accounts.

So let's look at each of the four points in more detail.

Cash & Ledgers

Cash and ledgers represent the entry point in the transaction flow. Every transaction your business engages in will be captured in either your cashbook or a ledger. This is covered in more detail in the next chapter but it's important to understand that these are the mechanisms by which a transaction enters the business and is first recorded.

Assets & Liabilities

All the individual transactions captured in your cashbook and ledgers are balanced at the end of the period. Ultimately all the income and expenditure which is not paid for in the period in which it is incurred or generated, will give rise to a timing difference. As seen in the previous chapter, any timing differences will therefore result in an asset or liability, which balances against the transactions captured in point one. We looked at some simple examples (ie purchase invoices and sales invoices) in the previous chapter, but this will be explored in more complex situations in Chapter 13.

Reporting

Once the balancing of transactions is complete and the Management Accounts have been created, the results are distilled into reports, to be reviewed by relevant parties within the business. The most important report, as previously alluded to, is the Management Accounts Pack itself. This is the key diagnostic evaluation document, pointing the reader in the direction of any deviations from the expected performance. However, this is only the beginning of the reporting process and in-depth analysis should be carried out, primarily by analysing variances and marginal contribution. In many cases, supporting reports will be created and these will also feature in the Management Accounts Pack, giving context and more detail around the key performance metrics within the business.

External Factors

After analysing variances and their potential causes, as well as scrutinising margin analysis, the directors should have the necessary data to evaluate the position of the business in the economic environment. This should enable them team to ascertain whether the current level of performance is adequate to sustain the business, at least as far as the end of the current plan. This evaluation should consider known risks and opportunities, as well as any potential external events and their impact on the business.

Pulling the Concepts Together

As you can see from the diagram below, executing the Four Points of

Control effectively will enable you to achieve the three Elements of Control as set out in Chapter 4. The first two points will give you flawless Performance Evaluation, while points three and four will assess your Economic Viability and Compliance.

The accuracy of your Performance Evaluation is critical and the Four Points of Control are the key touchpoints that ensure you get it right. If your Management Accounts are inaccurate, you may understate or overstate your Economic Viability and make inappropriate decisions for the following period.

However, this is where the cyclical nature of our framework comes into its own. Running your evaluation processes on a monthly basis makes it less likely that errors will impact your business to any significant extent. If you screw up in one month, the likelihood is that the error will be discovered the following month and any damage will be minimal.

The important thing to remember is that this entire framework requires accountability and discipline to work, which is the reason I advocate the facilitation stage. Engineering the conditions and culture which will give you the best change of successful implementation is a vital step which must not be skipped.

Producing monthly Management Accounts to cover off your Performance Evaluation, using additional reporting to rectify any problems (or maximise successes) diagnosed by the Management Accounts and consistently scanning and addressing external concerns is a painstaking process. But the good news is that it needn't be expensive and it yields massive rewards in terms of profit and longevity.

So now that we've explored the concepts of Financial Control, let's look at the processes and techniques by which it's achieved.

The Transaction Gateway

Cash and ledgers are the entry point for transactions in your business. This is where individual transactions are captured and recorded, before transitioning through the business and eventually settling as part of your profit.

Cash

'Cash' doesn't just refer to your bank balance or the amount of money in your petty cash tin. It means anything that could be considered a liquid financial resource. PayPal balance, gift vouchers, credit cards, cheques or anything else that can be used to make or receive an instant payment.

Cash – The Transaction Gateway

The receipt and expenditure of cash is captured in your cash book. Historically this was an actual book. The old-fashioned kind, made of actual paper. An accountant or book-keeper would record cash transactions in a lined book, with columns showing the transaction date, whether the money was going in or out, the value of the transaction and the party paying or receiving the cash.

Of course things have moved on since those days and although cash books still exist, they are mostly maintained electronically, either in a spreadsheet or a computerised, often cloud-based, system. However, the purpose of a cash book remains the same. To record cash transactions.

You may think this is no longer necessary, since we now have online banking, smartphone apps and integrated bank feeds. You can now check your bank balance instantly, make payments or view a statement with one tap. However, this will still only give you your bank balance. It won't give you the foresight to know what's coming in or going out.

Maintaining a cashbook is vital because there are situations where a cash payment or receipt will be recognised in your accounting system before it 'clears' into your bank account. An obvious example is a cheque, although cheques are a diminishing concern nowadays. But there are other examples, which are not going away anytime soon. For example, let's say a customer pays for an order using a debit card. You can't process the customer's order until payment is logged on the system, so you need to post the payment immediately, even though it won't actually clear into your bank account for a couple of days. When you post the payment, it's 'posted' into the 'Bank' account in your accounting system and therefore increases your bank balance. However, if you run a bank statement at this point, it won't agree to your accounting system. Now imagine you have a large e-commerce company and this is happening hundreds of times every day.

Your cash book is essentially the 'middle-man' between your bank statement and your accounting system. A periodic (daily, weekly or monthly, depending on the size and complexity of the business) reconciliation between all three is needed to ensure that everything has been captured and a reliable cash position can be established. Ultimately, every cash transaction must be captured in your cash book and reconciled to the accounting system. As long as this is done daily, you can check it against your bank statement less frequently, just to make sure everything is in sync.

Recognition of Costs and Revenue

As explored in part one of this book, the Accrual Accounting Convention sets out clear guidance as to when revenue and costs should be **recognised** in your accounting system. It also specifically states that the timing of cash flows should be ignored. It's important to understand that the date you actually pay an invoice has no bearing whatsoever on the date the cost is recognised in your accounts. This is a vital concept to grasp and it's one that many business owners, in my experience, struggle with, so let's use an example.

Let's say your business is exhibiting at a trade show in April and the primary intention is to generate sales leads. Remember that the Accrual Accounting Convention dictates that **the timing of costs should match to the timing of the revenue generated by those costs.** It's highly likely that you would have to pay some of the associated costs up front. A deposit to book the space at the show, the cost of manufacturing the stand and banners, a courier to deliver everything to the show, training for employees who will be manning the stand, parking permits for the day. All of these costs are likely to be invoiced before the date of the show.

Key dates are as follows:
- Exhibition date - 30th April 2021
- 50% Deposit payable to book the exhibition space - 15th January 2021
- 50% Balance for exhibition space - payable 25th April 2021
- Electrics, carpet, display stand, banners - Invoiced 12th April, payable on 31st May
- Parking permits - Purchased for cash on 29th April

All of these costs should be matched to the revenue generated by the show. This is the tricky bit because different shows, different industries and different businesses will have different timelines in terms of sales incubation. For the purposes of this example, we will assume that nothing is actually sold on the day of the show and it's purely a PR event.

The measurement of show-generated sales are not really the purpose of this book, but as a summary to support this exercise, here are some common approaches:

- Ask everyone who places an order how they heard about your company/service/product
- Use a code. Eg, "Quote this code when you order and you'll get a 5% discount". The code is only given to show attendees, so the company

can track sales generated from the show

- Estimate the projected sales based on the foot-fall at the exhibition

So let's assume when drafting our budget for the year that the show will yield a 20% increase in sales for the subsequent four months. The correct approach then would be to add together all the budgeted costs, **regardless of invoice dates or payment dates**, divide this total by four and enter this amount in your Sales & Marketing budget for the four months from May to August. The assumption here is that no sales prior to May can possibly be generated by this trade show, since it doesn't take place until 30th April. Any sales generated by the show will dissipate by the end of August so the total cost of the show must have been recognised by the end of August.

Profit vs Cash

From a cash point of view, things are very different. The deposit is payable in January, The stand and associated costs are payable in May and the parking permits are payable in April. You may also need to factor in hotels, lunches, fuel and other on-the-day costs. Failing to account for these items in your cash flow forecast will lead to cash pinch-points and breached overdrafts.

The point here is to recognise that recognition of revenues and expenses from an accounting point of view has nothing to do with the actual cash flow in relation to those revenues and expenses.

If you purchase stock on 1st April, receive the invoice for it on 2nd April and then sell it all on 12th April, your accounts will show purchases, sales and profit all in the same period.

However, the invoicing terms from your supplier are 60 days, so their invoice will not be paid until June. The credit terms extended to your customer are 90 days, so they won't have to pay you until July. None of this information is relevant when it comes to the recognition of revenue, costs or profit.

For this reason, it's vital to recognise the difference between:

- A budget - Expectation of revenues, expenses and profit in a period
- A cash flow forecast - Expectation of cash payments and receipts in a period

Ledgers - Management of Timing Differences

So what do we mean by 'ledgers' in this context. Ledgers are also known as 'Control Accounts' and are primarily used to recognise transactions which have not yet had any cash impact. Essentially they are used to manage timing differences such as credit terms.

In simple terms, the difference between a cash book and a ledger is as follows:

- Cash book - Measurement of cash paid or received (even if it hasn't actually impacted the bank balance yet)
- Ledgers - Measurement of amounts payable or receivable (at some point in the future)

Or to re-state this even more simply.

Ledgers = The recognition of an asset or liability
Cash = The settlement of an asset or liability

The most common ledgers are well known by most people in business - Purchase Ledger and Sales Ledger. These are also known by other names as follows:

Purchase Ledger: AKA Creditors Ledger, Creditors Control Account, Bought Ledger
Sales Ledger: AKA Debtors Ledger, Debtors Control Account or simply 'Debtors'

For the purposes of this book, we will stick with Purchase Ledger and Sales Ledger, but any of the above terms are acceptable.

Most business will have a Sales Ledger and Purchase Ledger, since most business offer credit terms to their customers and receive credit terms from their suppliers. A notable exception would be retail businesses, who rarely offer credit terms to customers, but even they will usually have credit accounts with suppliers. There are many other types of ledger (or Control Account) but we will start with the basics and work through an example.

Example: Cash Sale

So let's say we run a retail company selling shoes. We sell one pair of shoes for £200 and the customer pays on a debit card. The accounting entries for this are very simple:

Debit Bank account £200
Credit Sales account £200

Sales account				Bank account	
Debit	Credit			Debit	Credit
	Shoe sales £200			Shoe sales £200	

There's no need for a control account or ledger in this case, as there is no timing difference (apart from the minimal time taken for the debit card payment to reach your bank account). There is no need to recognise the asset (the money owed to you), as the payment was made instantly and no debt arose.

Example: Credit Sale

In the next example, our shoe retail operation has expanded into wholesale supply. We now have commercial customers, who expect credit terms. We have agreed 30 days terms on all purchases. So let's look at the accounting entries for this.

The sale still needs to be recognised at the point of invoice, so we will credit the Sales account. This part is exactly the same as in the first example. We can't recognise the increase in the bank balance at this point, as payment has not yet been made. But we can't post a debit without posting a credit, and we need to recognise the fact that we are now owed £200. So this is where the Sales Ledger comes into play.

Debit Sales Ledger £200
Credit Sales account £200

Sales account

Debit	Credit
	Shoe sales £200

Sales Ledger

Debit	Credit
Shoe sales £200	

This satisfies all requirements of the double entry accounting system and therefore the Accounting Equation. A new asset has been created, the sale has been recorded in the correct period and the countdown towards payment has started ticking.

Thirty days later, the customer settles the invoice and payment is received into the bank account. This is when we execute the second half of the transaction as follows:

Debit Bank account £200
Credit Sales Ledger £200

Sales Ledger

Debit	Credit
Shoe sales £200	Shoe sales £200

Bank account

Debit	Credit
Shoe sales £200	

This transaction clears the balance on the Sales Ledger, thereby settling the asset, while simultaneously increasing the bank balance by £200. The sale has been recorded in the correct period and the payment has been received into the bank. The eventual outcome is exactly the same as in the cash sale example, we just took a little longer to get there.

The full transaction is shown below. As you can see, if you ignore the account in the middle, the transactions on the Sales account and Bank account are exactly the same as in the Cash Sale example. This illustrates the role that Control Accounts play in the management of timing differences in transactions.

Sales account		Sales Ledger		Bank account	
Debit	Credit	Debit	Credit	Debit	Credit
	Shoe sales £200	Shoe sales £200	Shoe sales £200	Shoe sales £200	

Other Control Accounts

As mentioned above, Sales Ledger and Purchase Ledger are probably the two most common control accounts, but there are many others as follows:

- **VAT Control Account** - VAT is collected from customers and paid to suppliers, but the balance due to HMRC isn't paid over until a later date. The asset/liability must be recognised at the point of invoice and settled when paid over.
- **PAYE Control Account** - Income Tax/National Insurance Contributions are deducted from employees when they are paid, but paid to HMRC at a later date. This delay usually spans more than one period, so, again, this liability must be recognised while it exists.
- **Pension Control Account** - Pension contributions are deducted from employees but not paid to the pension company until a later date. Another liability to be recognised.
- **Amazon Seller Control Account** - When items are sold on Amazon (or other e-commerce platforms), often the platform itself will collect payment and pay it to the seller later on. This then becomes an asset to be recognised in the accounts of the seller.

This is still a relatively small selection of the potential control accounts which may apply to your business. Essentially, whenever there is a timing difference between the recognition of an asset or liability and the settlement of that asset or liability, you will need to use a control account to manage it.

I should reiterate at this point that my intention is not to turn my readers into accountants. Don't be put off by the technical detail in this chapter or elsewhere in this book. The vast majority of business owners who fail have a generally poor level of accounting knowledge and the relatively narrow scope of the technical accounting discussed in this book will stand you in good stead if you take the time to understand it. More than that, it's part of your accountability as a business owner to understand this, even if you delegate the actual processes to someone else.

You can expand on these concepts with a simple Google search if you would like to take your understanding to the next level, or you can book one-on-one Finance Coaching with PPX directly at https://ppxconsulting.co.uk

Capturing

Hopefully you can now see how and why Cash and Ledgers are the first point of control. With the exception of certain types of capital transaction, which are very rare in SMEs, every transaction in a business is captured in either a control account or a cash book, as shown in the list of examples below:

- Cash payment   -   Cash book
- Cash receipt   -   Cash book
- Sales invoice   -   Sales ledger
- Purchase invoice -   Purchase ledger
- HMRC returns   -   Control accounts
- Payroll   -   Control account/Cash book
- Proforma deposits -   Cash book
- Petty cash float   -   Cash book

Individual transactions in the period are captured in the cash book and ledgers and will ultimately appear in the P&L for the period, while assets and liabilities arising in the period are recorded in the balance sheet, as we will see in the next chapter.

Chapter 13 - Assets & Liabilities: Balancing

Assets & Liabilities

So what are assets and liabilities? I'm sure you know, but you also probably know by now that I like to add context.

Assets & Liabilities are ultimately the cumulative balances of any non-cash transactions, which have been recognised in previous periods but not yet settled. The more traditional definition, which is that *assets are owned by the business and that liabilities are owed by the business'* is also broadly true.

Some items are obviously assets or liabilities. For example a forklift owned by the company is an obvious asset, and a bank loan is obviously a liability. However, there are more obscure examples that are not instantly recognisable as either.

Accruals and Prepayments

As you may remember from Chapter 6, when we looked at accounting concepts and more specifically, the Accrual Accounting Convention, certain items need to be brought forward or pushed back in terms of timing, so that costs and revenues are recognised in the correct periods. We looked at examples of a prepayment (insurance invoice) and an accrual (electricity bill). Feel free to go back to Chapter 6 and refresh your memory, as we are about to touch on these examples again here.

The method by which accruals and prepayments are managed is similar to the method described in the previous chapter for managing timing differences on invoices. The Chart of Accounts in your accounting system will include a Prepayments account and an Accruals account, which are used in a similar way to the Control Accounts outlined in the previous chapter. For example the insurance invoice for £12,000 in the prepayments example we looked at would be debited directly to the Prepayments account in the first instance and then £1,000 per month would be 'reversed' out into your P&L, so that the cost was recognised in the correct periods and spread across the twelve months to which the insurance policy relates.

The Correct Calculation of Profit in a Period

The reason the timing of transactions is so important feeds into the very core of the Control Cycle. The correct calculation of profit, in terms of both timing and numerical accuracy, is **absolutely vital** if you hope to establish control of your business (I've used bold type because the phrase 'absolutely vital' is still not emphatic enough to highlight the importance of this concept)

Remember that:

- Without accurate profit, reliable performance evaluation is impossible
- Without reliable performance evaluation, it's impossible to assess economic viability
- Without accurate profit, compliance is impossible

So, in summary, without accurate profit calculations, it's impossible to establish control of your business.

Balancing

Remember the Accounting Equation:

$$Equity = (Assets - Liabilities)$$

As with all equations, the two sides need to balance. All the individual transactions which have been captured in point one of the Four Points of Control will have been classified as either:

- Asset
- Liability
- Income
- Expense

Since income and expenses are profit items and profit is included within Equity, we should now be able to deduct liabilities from assets to balance the Accounting Equation. So how is this done.

Obviously this is done through the correct processing of individual transactions in your accounting system, but how do you ensure that it's been done correctly?

Essentially the Balance Sheet does it for you. Every transaction which has ever impacted your business is accounted for here, until it's extracted from the business in the form of a dividend. All **Income** received and **Expenses** incurred are recorded in the Equity section, which all **Assets** and **Liabilities** are accounted for in the Net Assets section. As long as these two agree with each other, then the Accounting Equation works and everything balances.

This is where any transactions which were not settled in the period will reside. All ledgers, control accounts, accruals, prepayments, fixed assets, stock balances, goodwill, loan balances and any other items owned by, owed to, or owed by the business are recorded, along with their current balances as at the end of the period.

To make the balance sheet balance, you need to add in the equity and profit. This means it is literally the embodiment of the Accounting Equation and this is how it balances everything. All that remains to do is to prove these balances, which we will look at in more detail in Chapter 16.

Chapter 14 - Reporting: Analysing

How and Why

Once the Management Accounts have been produced, your Performance Evaluation is complete. The next step is to analyse this performance in order to assess your Economic Viability. The purpose of this is to establish **how** and **why** any deviations from the expected performance occurred.

Although the Management Accounts will tell you where to look for these deviations, they won't usually give you the detail you need in order to investigate further. This is where additional reporting is required.

It's important to ensure that both negatives and positives are reviewed and analysed. It's natural to investigate failure to understand what went wrong, but too often the reasons for success go unquestioned. The general stance is that if something went better than expected, that's great, so don't question it. But the truth is that all deviations should be investigated and understood to the greatest extent possible, so that positives can be maximised and nasty surprises can be minimised or avoided entirely. Apart from that, it's sometimes the case that the unexpected success is actually an error, which is only discovered if you investigate further.

Variance Analysis

By far the most useful function of the Management Accounts is comparative reporting and the analysis of variances against budgeted performance. Variance Analysis is a vital concept to understand and a key skill to master, as this is the method by which you can understand the actual reason for variances and therefore do something about them.

The extract shown below is similar to the examples we reviewed in Chapter 7, when we looked at Performance Evaluation in more detail. In this example, you can see that the majority of the variances are in line with budgeted expectations, in that their increase is proportionately in line with the increase in sales revenue The theory here is that if sales revenue increases, then activity must have increased and therefore an increase in cost is to be expected. However, there are a few key deviations which are not proportionate, as shown by the significant difference between budgeted Gross

Margin (59.6%) and actual Gross Margin (43.4%).

	Actual January		Budget January		Variance
	PROFIT & LOSS - JANUARY				
REVENUE					
Transport Income	373,835		265,000		108,835
Other Income	0		0		0
Total Revenue	373,835		265,000		108,835
COST OF SALES					
Direct Labour	38,126	10.2%	27,000	10.2%	(11,126)
Fuel	134,581	36.0%	55,000	20.8%	(79,581)
Fleet Maintenance	10,640	2.8%	7,500	2.8%	(3,140)
Subcontractors	9,624	2.6%	4,000	1.5%	(5,624)
Fleet Insurances	12,768	3.4%	9,000	3.4%	(3,768)
Tyres	4,522	1.2%	3,500	1.3%	(1,022)
Operators & Vehicle Licences	1,330	0.4%	1,000	0.4%	(330)
Total Cost of Sales	211,591	56.6%	107,000	40.4%	(104,591)
GROSS PROFIT	162,244		158,000		4,244
Gross profit margin	43.4%		59.6%		

The variances to investigate are as follows, as these are the only figures which materially deviate from budgeted amounts/percentages.

Sales: Budgeted sales revenue = £265k Actual sales revenue £374k. Sales Revenue is therefore 41% up on budget

Fuel: Budgeted as 20.8% of sales, actually 36% of sales. This means that the increase in fuel cost is greater than that which would be expected purely in relation to additional activity.

Subcontractors: Budgeted as 1.5% of sales, actually 2.6% of sales. Again this means the increase is not proportionate based solely on increased revenue.

Once you have established that variances exist, you must analyse them to establish **how** and **why** they have occurred, so that you can either make changes to eradicate them, or adjust your expectations going forward. To do this, you need to examine the composite elements of that cost. This is the first step in Variance Analysis.

Cost of Sales (or 'direct costs') almost always consist of at least two composite elements. This is different when dealing with overheads, because overheads do not relate directly to output and are therefore not a proportionate cost in relation to sales revenue. Direct costs, on the other hand, must always relate to the level of output, otherwise they are not truly direct costs. This relationship is the reason there are always composite elements.

So what do I mean by composite elements? Let's work through the variances identified above and this will become clear.

Sales variance: The total variance is £108,835 (373,835 actual - 265,000 budget) and since the actual result was higher than the budgeted result, this is know as a **favourable** variance.

The only explanations for higher sales revenue are as follows:

1. We sold more products than we expected to
2. We sold products for a higher price than we expected to
3. Some combination of 1 and 2 above

This means that the composite elements are **sales price** and **volume.** Therefore, to establish the reason for the dramatic increase in sales revenue, we need to analyse these two composite variances.

The business in question is a courier operation, delivering goods on behalf of e-commerce companies. So let's say that, when the budget was compiled for the year, the sales budget for January was based on making 2,000 deliveries at an average price of £132.50 per delivery.

132.50 x 2,000 = £265,000, hence the budgeted sales revenue for January.

To ascertain what led to the favourable variance, we need to understand how many deliveries were actually made in January and the average price charged. After running a sales report for the period from the transport system, we have determined that actually, we made 4,200 deliveries in the month, but the average price was £89.01 (89.0083333 rounded).

89.0083333 x 4,200 = 373,835, hence the actual sales revenue for January

From this, we can calculate the composite variances and begin our investigation:

Sales volume variance = Additional volume sold (2,200) x budgeted selling price (132.50)
2,200 x 132.50 = 291,500, which is a **favourable** variance, since sales **volume** was higher than expected (4,200 deliveries compared to 2,000 deliveries)

Sales price variance = Difference between actual and budgeted sales price (132.50 - 89.0083333 = 43.4916667) x actual sales volume (4,200)
43.4916667 x 4,200 = 182,665, which is an **adverse** variance (as the selling price was lower than budgeted).

When the two composite variances are added together, they should equal the total variance.

Sales volume variance: £291,500 (Favourable)
Sales price variance: -£182,665 (Adverse)
Total variance: (291,500 - 182,665) = £108,835 (Favourable)

This is a good example of why it's important to analyse positives as well as negatives. In this case, we have smashed our sales budget by over 40%, but after further analysis, we have established that our actual selling price is considerably lower than our budgeted selling price. We have counteracted this by increasing volumes in this period, but if volumes drop off next month and we haven't understood the reason for the lower selling price, we may be left scratching our heads and making a loss.

Once the variance has been analysed, the next step is to ascertain why the selling price was so much lower than expected and how the volume sold was so much higher. This is achieved through supporting reports, which we will discuss later in the chapter.

Now that we've analysed the sales variance, this just leaves the two cost variances: Fuel and Subcontractors.

Fuel variance: Similarly, the only way a fuel variance can exist is if we either used more fuel than expected, or paid more per litre for the fuel, or some combination of the two. Therefore, the composite variances are **Fuel price** and **Fuel usage.** We can calculate the composite variances in the same way as we did for the sales variances and ascertain whether we used too much fuel or paid higher prices than expected.

Subcontractors variance: Subcontractors are a direct labour cost, so the relevant variables will be the hourly rate paid and the number of hours used. Therefore the composite variances will be **Subcontractor rate** variance or **Subcontractor efficiency** variance. This can be calculated in the same way as the previous examples. It's important to remember that all direct costs are ultimately a resource cost, whether it's raw material, labour hours, consumables or anything else.

The key points to remember here are as follows:

1. When compiling your budget, it's important to calculate revenues and direct costs with reference to prices and volumes, otherwise it will be difficult to analyse variances at a later date. Your revenue budget should consist of a volume estimate and a selling price, where possible. Your budgeted direct costs should consist of expected usage (eg number of hours/litres/metres/units) and expected cost per unit used.

2. It's important to analyse the composite variances and look for reasons why they have occurred, whether positive or negative. Remember that you need accurate data to make key decisions and that data can only be the result of robust analysis and supporting reports.

3. The overall variance is the total of the composite variances. Even if the overall variance is adverse or favourable, the individual composite variances could be a mixture, as in the sales variance example we worked through earlier in this chapter. It's important to analyse both composite variances in case one is masking the impact of the other.

4. Most direct costs will be made up of at least two composite elements, such as price and volume. If this is not the case, they're probably not truly direct costs and maybe overheads classified incorrectly. For example, rent (an overhead) will be the same cost, regardless of sales volume. Material costs will fluctuate in line with sales, since material will only be used in the manufacture of product for sale.

Supporting Reports

Once the variances have been analysed and the mathematical reasons for deviations are understood, the next step is to investigate why they have occurred. For example we have established that the sales volume in January was more than double the budgeted sales volume, but that the average sales price was considerably lower than budgeted. After running sales reports and discussing further internally, it has come to light that one of the company's sales reps had agreed a price reduction in order to secure a large contract, which resulted in a dramatic increase in sales volume for one month only. This means that everything should return to normal the following month and there is no cause for concern.

Similarly, the adverse variances on fuel and subcontractor costs can be investigated further by running fuel usage reports, reviewing fuel card invoices/petrol station receipts, rates agreed with subcontractors and reports from the clocking in machine. These reports are collectively known as supporting reports.

Where supporting reports are used, they must agree to the totals in the Management Accounts. For example, we know that the 'Subcontractors' cost in the period was £9,624, because that's what the Management Accounts say. Bear in mind that by the time we produce the Management Accounts, all transactions have been captured and balanced, so we can have faith that they are correct. Therefore, if the supporting reports say anything other than £9,624, they are probably incorrect and the reason for this discrepancy should be understood before any further analysis is carried out.

Supporting reports should form part of your general monthly reporting framework. Don't wait until you have an issue to resolve before you create them, as there may be a historical trend which has led to the current issue. The more data you produce to accompany your Management Accounts, the more effectively you will be able to investigate and resolve a problem.

Examples of typical supporting reports are as follows:

- Sales reports
- Labour analysis reports (not necessarily financial)
- KPI reporting
- Score cards
- Stock usage reports

Breakeven Analysis

The next step after Variance Analysis is Breakeven Analysis. Essentially the company will 'break even' when Gross Profit is equal to overheads, so Breakeven Profit is the same as the overheads for the month and Breakeven sales revenue (also known as the 'Breakeven Point') is therefore defined as:

Total Overheads / Gross Profit Margin

From the example below, we can see that the budgeted total overheads were £145,250 and the budgeted Gross Margin percentage is 59.6%. So to calculate the Breakeven Point:

145,250 / 59.6% = 243,615.50

So to break even in January, assuming the budgeted gross margin remains constant and overheads are budgeted accurately, we would need sales revenue of £243,615.50.

	PROFIT & LOSS - JANUARY			
	Actual January		Budget January	Variance
REVENUE				
Transport Income	373,835		265,000	108,835
Other Income	0		0	0
Total Revenue	373,835		265,000	108,835
COST OF SALES				
Direct Labour	38,126	10.2%	27,000 10.2%	(11,126)
Fuel	134,581	36.0%	55,000 20.8%	(79,581)
Fleet Maintenance	10,640	2.8%	7,500 2.8%	(3,140)
Subcontractors	9,624	2.6%	4,000 1.5%	(5,624)
Fleet Insurances	12,768	3.4%	9,000 3.4%	(3,768)
Tyres	4,522	1.2%	3,500 1.3%	(1,022)
Operators & Vehicle Licences	1,330	0.4%	1,000 0.4%	(330)
Total Cost of Sales	211,591	56.6%	107,000 40.4%	(104,591)
GROSS PROFIT	162,244		158,000	4,244
Gross profit margin	43.4%		59.6%	
OVERHEADS				
Administrative Salaries	63,540	17.0%	63,500 24.0%	(40)
Insurances	19,322	5.2%	19,750 7.5%	428
Accountancy & Audit fees	9,042	2.4%	9,000 3.4%	(42)
Bank Charges	950	0.3%	1,000 0.4%	50
Legal & Professional	7,490	2.0%	7,500 2.8%	10
Printing & Stationery	2,075	0.6%	2,000 0.8%	(75)
Telephone & Internet	3,425	0.9%	3,500 1.3%	75
Training	4,950	1.3%	5,000 1.9%	50
Depreciation	13,300	3.6%	13,000 4.9%	(300)
Computer Expenses	2,491	0.7%	2,500 0.9%	9
Subsistence	3,230	0.9%	3,000 1.1%	(230)
Uniforms & Protective Clothing	2,533	0.7%	2,500 0.9%	(33)
Advertising & Promotional Costs	10,827	2.9%	11,000 4.2%	173
Health & Safety	1,950	0.5%	2,000 0.8%	50
Total Overhead costs	145,125	54.3%	145,250 54.8%	125
Overhead %age	38.8%		54.8%	
Total Overheads & Cost of Sales	356,715	133.6%	252,250 95.2%	(104,465)
Net Profit	17,120	6.4%	12,750 4.8%	4,370
Net profit margin	4.6%		4.8%	

The difference between your budgeted sales revenue and your breakeven sales revenue is known as your 'Margin of Safety'. This is the degree to which you can afford to miss your sales budget without making a loss. To calculate your Margin of Safety:

Margin of Safety =
((Budgeted Sales Revenue - Breakeven Sales Revenue) / Budgeted Sales Revenue) x 100

So using the example above, the calculation would be as follows:

((265,000 - 243,615.50) / 265,000) x 100

= (21,384 / 265,000) x 100

= 8.07%

This means we could afford for sales to drop by up to 8.07% before we would make a loss, assuming budgeted overheads and Gross Margin were accurate.

Breakeven Analysis is a vital part of assessing your Economic Viability and making decisions that impact the profitability of the business. It can be used in conjunction with Variance Analysis to forecast problems, decide on remedial action or support with future budgeting.

For example, once we have analysed the three variances identified above, we can then incorporate changes in gross margin percentage into our Breakeven calculation and determine the long-term effect of any variances. Similarly, if we lose a repeat customer and we can reliably estimate the drop in sales revenue resulting from this, we can measure the impact on our Breakeven Point just by amending the budgeted sales revenue used in the Breakeven analysis. If we know we can afford to drop 8% of sales and still break even, then it's a simple matter to ascertain whether the drop in sales from losing the aforementioned customer is more or less than 8% and therefore what the damage will be to the bottom line profit. It also allows for experimentation of pricing changes, incentivisation of sales staff, setting cost-reduction targets and other initiatives.

In the context of Financial Control, we don't need to dig any deeper into this concept, but Breakeven Reporting is a very powerful tool and includes wider economic concepts such as marginal contribution, price elasticity and analysis of gross margins.

Analysing

As already alluded to, Reporting is the third point of control and is focused on analysing the transactions captured in the first point and balanced in the second point. This analysis is then carried forward into the fourth and final point of control, External Factors, where we will evaluate the business in the context of the economic environment.

Chapter 15 - External Factors: Evaluating

Sustainability

When assessing the Economic Viability of a business, you need to consider current viability, which is ascertained from the Management Accounts, but also future viability, otherwise known as sustainability. Even if your business is highly profitable and entirely controllable, the external landscape can shift without warning and undermine your operation. For this reason, sustainability can only truly be assessed if you factor in the external environment.

But the external environment is a pretty big place, so where do we start?

All business will have their unique external sensitivities, depending on the industry and market they operate in. However, there are four factors which are universal and will impact all organisations, so let's start there.

1. **Market** - The market in which the business operates.
2. **Behaviours** - Customer behaviours and the forces that influence them
3. **External regulation** - HMRC, legislation, affiliations and accreditations etc
4. **External events** - Recession, war, interest rate movements, natural disasters etc

Obviously some of these are easier to predict than others, but the main characteristic they all have in common is that they are outside the control of the organisation. The only element of control available is the nature and extent of your reaction. For this reason they need to be classified and assessed in terms of risk and opportunity.

This chapter deals with subjective concepts and it will be impossible for me to give you a strategy for dealing with the specific risks and events faced by your business. However, the Four Points of Control framework advocates a systematic approach for identifying and managing risks, which should be adaptable to any business. This starts with the four main factors listed above, so let's look at them in more detail.

1. Market

Understanding the market in which the business operates is crucial to understanding your viability. The market factors you should consider are as follows:

- Size - How big is the market, in terms of value or spend, and what is your current market share. Is there scope to increase that share? If so, how can you achieve that?
- Products - What products are available within your chosen market and how do your products compare? What is the short, medium and long term demand for your products and services?
- Competitors - Who else is in your market and what are they doing the same/differently to you. Are you in a position to compete with them, or do you even need to compete with them?

2. Behaviours

What forces drive your customers to you? What customer need does your product fulfil and what stops your customers from buying elsewhere. What do you need to do to ensure that your customers come to you time and time again. How can you quantify the risk of your customers no longer needing your product, or being able to obtain it elsewhere.

3. External Regulation

What regulation exists in your industry and what do you need to do in order to comply with it? Do you fully understand your obligations under legal and governmental rules? Are there any obligations that don't currently apply but may apply as the business grows? Are you aware of the thresholds for this and when you expect to breach them? Are there any optional affiliations or certifications you could achieve that would give you a competitive advantage?

4. External Events

Hard to predict, but potentially the most damaging, external events can come from anywhere and wreak havoc. Having said that, they rarely arrive without warning signs, so we will explore this in more detail later in this chapter.

The four factors described above are common to all businesses. All businesses operate within a market, all have customers, all have to comply with external regulation and are all vulnerable to external events. Most of the external factors a business needs to consider could come under one of these headings, but there are others.

Discuss this in more detail with your colleagues and team members to see if there are any external risks or opportunities which fall outside of these categories and come up with a plan to manage them. Possible additional factors could include:

- Supply chain
- Technology
- Expansion of capabilities
- Legislation
- Budget constraints

Unfortunately, there is always a possibility that something unforeseen could impact your business, so the real countermeasure you need to perfect is to be ready for anything. The best way to increase readiness is to remember the 'Braking Distance' principle I keep talking about, as well as another favourite concept of mine - Scanning the horizon.

Scanning the Horizon

As the name suggests, scanning the horizon simply means keeping yourself informed of…,well, pretty much everything that may affect your business, whether directly or indirectly. Sign up to industry forums and mailing lists, read trade publications, stay abreast of world news, communicate with your network. This may seem like hard work but it's the only way to ensure that all bases are covered. In the wake of the COVID-19 pandemic, I have heard many business owners say "No one saw that coming" but that's not strictly true. Many businesses were prepared for a pandemic and some were specifically prepared for COVID-19, or something like it. Many larger businesses have plans for almost any potential scenario, including pandemics, terrorist attacks, recessions, even nuclear war. Of course these are generally large corporate organisations who have the staffing and budget to assign teams of people to business resiliency. This book is aimed at SMEs and smaller businesses and I'm not advocating that you take this kind of action, but you still have a responsibility to mitigate the impact of external events to whatever extent you can.

Generally-speaking, the external factors you need to consider come under two broad categories.

1. **Ongoing sensitivities** - The external influences your business is subject to on a regular basis, as part of your normal operational activities. This would include such things as currency exchange rates, commodity prices, labour rates and regulatory activities, such as audits.
2. **External events** - Events which may affect your business when or if they happen, but are unlikely to be a regular occurrence. In this case, rather than monitoring the impact and incorporating it into your long-term strategy, you just need to gauge and mitigate the risk.

These two different types of influence should be managed in different ways

Weighted Sensitivity Metrics

Ongoing sensitivities need to be monitored on a periodic basis, as changes could have a significant influence on your profit levels and therefore impact your Economic Viability. Let's look at a practical example:

SonicWear Ltd - (an Entirely Fictional Business)

SonicWear Ltd is a clothing wholesaler buying 100% cotton t shirts in bulk and selling to other businesses (as opposed to consumers). They sell plain t shirts in various colours. Their product is not bespoke or unique, so they need to be consistently competitive on price. All stock is purchased directly from manufacturers in China and they are subject to large minimum order quantities in order to keep their purchase prices as low as possible. Sonicwear's customers generally expect at least 30 days credit terms, but their chinese suppliers must be paid before shipment. Payment to suppliers is made in US dollars. All product is shipped by ocean freight in order to keep costs down. Terms with their suppliers are ex-works, not FOB, so they have to arrange collection and customs clearance independently.

Based on the summary of this business, we can deduce that they are susceptible to the following sensitivity metrics:

1. Cotton Price - Although they don't purchase the raw material directly, the cotton price will undoubtedly affect the price charged by their suppliers.
2. Exchange rates - The company is based in the UK but pays suppliers in USD. Changes in the exchange rate could have a significant impact on profit.
3. Selling price/Competition - The market is very competitive and the product is not unique, so monitoring competitors' prices is important.
4. Customs legislation - The company is responsible for arranging shipping and customs clearance, so changes to legislation could lead to additional costs or delays.
5. Weather/Shipping conditions - All product is shipped by ocean freight, so delays due to weather are a possibility.
6. Chinese new year - Many Chinese businesses close down for a significant period for Chinese New Year, so the company will need to plan orders and shipping dates accordingly to avoid running out of stock.

These six external metrics will be a factor as long as SonicWear continues to operate in this way. Therefore they will need to form part of the monthly reporting package and the long-term strategy. Any changes in the metrics should be assessed for their impact. Some of these factors will be easier to manage than others. For example, the date of the Chinese New Year will be known and can therefore be planned for, whereas a typhoon in the South China Sea may be harder to predict.

Weighting

Once the sensitivity metrics have been identified, they should be graded in order of sensitivity or severity. I have ranked the metrics above in this order, with the cotton price being the most impactful and Chinese New Year the least serious. This isn't always a clear-cut ranking and may be a matter of debate among the directors of the business. Also, it may be that the ranking changes over time. For example, if the cotton price is currently very low and shows no likelihood of increasing in the near future but exchange rates are currently soaring, you may decide that the weighting needs to change in favour of the most volatile metric.

The purpose of weighting is to apply appropriate focus to the metrics that matter. If customs legislation is currently under review, this may be cause for concern, but if the cotton price is also on the rise, this should be the main topic under discussion. Once a strategy to mitigate the impact of the cotton price has been agreed, then the customs legislation can be considered.

Event Tiers

The approach for external events is different. The assumption is that these events are a one-off and once the business has dealt with them, they are unlikely to be repeated in the near future. If they are regular events (such as Chinese New Year), then they should be considered as an ongoing sensitivity, as opposed to an external event.

The approach to these events is more a case of assessing the risk and then 'riding it out' as best you can. If an external event starts to become a regular occurrence, then it may be more appropriate to add it to your list of ongoing sensitivities and review it accordingly.

To measure and manage the risk of external events, the key is, as mentioned earlier, to be well-informed. The earlier you become aware of a potential event, the better you can assess the risk and come up with a plan. To monitor the approach of an external event and grade the potential risk, you can use an 'Event Tiers' model, as shown below:

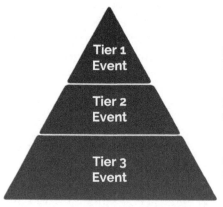

Tier 1 Event — **Most concern** – Has happened or will certainly happen. Will definitely affect the business.

Tier 2 Event — **Moderate concern** – Has happened or will certainly happen. May affect the business.

Tier 3 Event — **Least concern** – Hasn't yet happened, may not happen at all. Assess the potential impact.

As the model suggests, a Tier 1 Event will definitely happen and will definitely affect the business, so the risk needs to be assessed and managed. A Tier 3 Event may have been identified but at this stage it's uncertain as to whether it will definitely happen and, even if it does, it may not affect the business. This event will need to be monitored regularly in case it begins to creep up the pyramid.

Risk Matrices

Once an event has been identified and assigned to a Tier, the risk should be assessed. A reliable method of assessing risks is to use a Risk Matrix, like the one shown below.

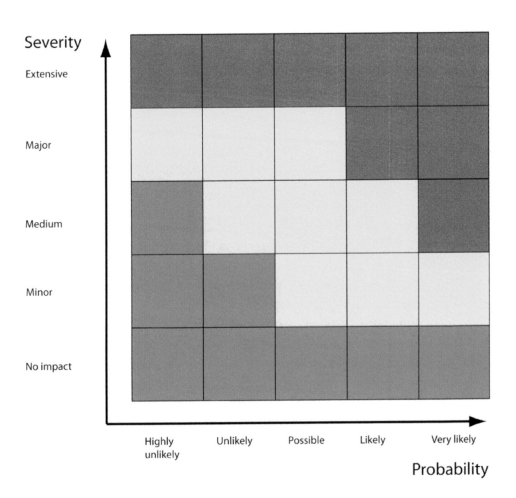

A risk matrix takes into account the likelihood and severity of the event and grades it accordingly. The red section of the matrix denotes an unacceptable risk, which means a strategy to reduce or avoid the impact would need to be formulated. The green section suggests that the event is not likely to cause significant disruption and no specific plan is required. The yellow section would need to be discussed further and the benefits of taking action would have to be weighed against the resources required to formulate and implement a plan.

Risk Registers

A Risk Register is an important tool in any business. This is a record of the main risks facing the business and a record of the potential impact, the measures in place to mitigate or avoid the risk, the person responsible for managing the risk (if applicable) and the scale of the risk. A risk register should certainly include any ongoing sensitivities but may also include external events if they are considered significant.

Business Resilience

All of the concepts and activities outlined in this chapter should culminate in a robust business resilience plan. This should incorporate the following plans and initiatives:

- **Resilience Schedule** - Risks facing the business, emergency contact list, general ongoing security measures (such as data back up) and how they are carried out.
- **Crisis Planning Schedule** - What to do when things go wrong. This should include plans for emergency situations, such as a fire or cyber attack and instructions for all employees.
- **Disaster Recovery Plan** - What to do after a serious event, where normal conditions have been disrupted. This should include emergency contacts information, relocation information and plans for business continuity

Evaluating

So that's the last of the Four Points of Control. The purpose of this point is to use the data generated in the first three points, where transactions are captured, balanced and then analysed to evaluate the business in the context of the external economic environment.

By the time this has been carried out, you should have achieved Performance Evaluation, assessed your Economic Viability and ensured your Compliance. In other words, you have achieved control of your business.

Chapter 16 - Control Mechanisms

Measurement of Control

We've looked at the way control is established in a business but, so far, to be perfectly honest, we've seen nothing that stops you forcing things to balance and no reason you can't fabricate reports to say anything you want. I've said that the Balance Sheet is the anchor of the P&L because the total of the P&L must agree to the profit shown in the Balance Sheet. But surely you can just type in any numbers you need to in order to force it to agree to the Balance Sheet?

That's why we have Control Mechanisms.

Control Mechanisms

As business owners or directors, Control Mechanisms are the area, more than any other process in this book, where your focus should be directed. All of the other processes outlined in Part Two of this book are the domain of your accountant or your in-house Finance team.

Control Mechanisms, however, are the method you, as senior management, can use to challenge what you're presented with.

Each of the Four Points of Control have an associated Control Mechanism. The purpose of these mechanisms is two-fold:

1. To verify the numbers used in the P&L and Balance Sheet
2. To measure the extent of control achieved

So let's look at the Control Mechanism for each of the Four Points of Control

Control Point	Control Mechanism
Cash & Ledgers	Reconciliations
Assets & Liabilities	Schedules
Reporting	Relevance, Impartiality, Accuracy
External Factors	Weighted Sensitivity Metrics

Cash & Ledgers - Reconciliation to Independent Data

This is where transactions are first captured, so it would stand to reason that if all transactions are verified at this point, the rest of the Transaction Flow should take care of itself. For this reason, this is where the most meticulous and reliable verification takes place. The control mechanism for Cash & Ledgers is **Reconciliation to Independent Data**. Independent, in this context, means external data from an independent source. Reconciliation of internal data to other internal data from the same system isn't reliable, in fact you could say that it's not really reconciliation at all.

So what independent data are we talking about?

The document below is an extract from a bank statement. This is obviously independent information, since it has been issued by an external party (the bank) and can't be influenced by anyone internally.

Statement

DATE	TYPE	IN	OUT	END OF DAY ACCOUNT BALANCE
	OPENING BALANCE			£0.00
05/01/2021	FASTER PAYMENT	£600.00		£600.00
06/01/2021	CHIP & PIN		£11.00	£589.00
08/01/2021	FASTER PAYMENT		£250.00	
08/01/2021	ONLINE PAYMENT		£13.00	
08/01/2021	CONTACTLESS		£37.00	£289.00
10/01/2021	FASTER PAYMENT		£280.00	£9.00
11/01/2021	CONTACTLESS		£4.25	
11/01/2021	CARD PAYMENT	£20.70		
11/01/2021	CONTACTLESS		£4.25	£21.20
12/01/2021	FASTER PAYMENT	£1500.00		£1521.20
13/01/2021	CONTACTLESS		£5.50	
13/01/2021	FASTER PAYMENT		£139.85	£1375.85

The document below is an extract from the company's internal cash book. If you compare the two documents you will see that the opening balance of £0.00 and the closing balance of £1,375.85 match exactly. Not only that but if there were any discrepancies in the closing balance, we would be able to review the individual transactions in order to find it. This is therefore a reconciliation to an external document and proves conclusively that the individual transactions have been recorded correctly in our system.

Receipts					Payments			
Date	Details	Total	Sales ledger		Date	Details	Total	Balance
05-Jan	Sales receipts (INV-5201)	600.00	600.00		05-Jan	Trf to Reserves	250.00	350.00
		0.00			06-Jan	Wickes	11.00	339.00
		0.00			07-Jan	Wickes	37.00	302.00
		0.00			07-Jan	Companies House	13.00	289.00
		0.00			10-Jan	Trf to Reserves	280.00	9.00
		0.00			11-Jan	Starbucks	4.25	4.75
		0.00			11-Jan	Wickes (Refund)	-20.70	25.45
		0.00			11-Jan	Starbucks	4.25	21.20
13-Jan	Sales receipts (INV-5207)	1,500.00	1,500.00		13-Jan	Starbucks	5.50	1,515.70
		0.00			13-Jan	Employee expenses	139.85	1,375.85

So that's an example of a cash reconciliation, but transactions can also be recorded in ledgers, so how do we verify those.

The extract below is taken from a supplier account statement. Again, this is issued by an external party (the supplier) so can't be influenced by anyone internally.

DATE	DESCRIPTION	CHARGES	CREDITS	ACCOUNT BALANCE
	Balance brought forward	£0.00		£0.00
01/10/2021	Invoice 04602 September 2021	£1,800.00		£1,800.00
01/11/2021	Invoice 04701 October 2021	£1,800.00		£3,600.00
01/12/2021	Invoice 04884 November 2021	£1,800.00		£5,400.00

Below is a report from the internal accounting system, showing the Purchase Ledger account for the same supplier. As you can see, the total balance of £5,400 matches exactly to the supplier's statement. You can see that there are multiple invoices for the same amount, which is often the case, as some suppliers will provide the same product or service multiple times, for the same price. For this reason, it's important to check that the invoice numbers that make up the balance are also in agreement. You can see from the two documents that this is the case, so everything matches perfectly.

01/10/2021	Invoice 04602 September 2021	£1,800.00
01/11/2021	Invoice 04701 October 2021	£1,800.00
01/12/2021	Invoice 04884 November 2021	£1,800.00
	Account balance	£5,400.00

In theory, every number on the P&L should be subject to this reconciliation process where possible. Sometimes it's simply not possible, for example, you can't force a supplier to issue a statement, but every attempt should be made to carry out a reconciliation to independent (external) data.

Assets & Liabilities - Balance Schedules

The control mechanism for Assets & Liabilities is **Balance Schedules**. Balance schedules take the reconciled numbers from the first point of control and compile them as totals. Those totals are then matched to the balances of assets and liabilities on the balance sheet.

In the example on the next page, you can see that the total cash balance ('Bank and cash equivalents) is shown in the Balance Sheet as £42,887. The associated balance schedule on the right hand side (which has been extracted from the accounting system) shows the same total at the bottom.

Balance Sheet: July 2021	Jul-21
Fixed Assets	
Fixed assets - Office Equipment	3,582
Fixed assets - Plant & Machinery	14,856
Fixed assets - Motor Vehicles	9,855
Total Fixed Assts	28,293
Current Assets	
Accounts Receivable	27,856
Bank and cash equivalents	42,887
Prepayments	5,246
Other current assets	452
Total Current Assets	76,441
Current Liabilities	
Accounts Payable	18,542
Accruals	11,244
PAYE Payable	2,585
VAT Liability	8,542
Pension contributions payable	845
Other current liabilities	642
Total Current Liabilities	42,400
Long Term Liabilities	
Loans	8,528
Hire purchase	1,419
Total Long Term Liabilities	9,947
NET ASSETS	52,387
Funded by:	
Current year profit	16,543
Retained Earnings	35,844
EQUITY	52,387

Schedule of cash balances

Current account 1	38,442.12
Current account 2	1,375.85
EUR bank account	2,106.44
Paypal account	962.81
Total	42,887.22

Creditors Control Account

Supplier A	1,276.64
Supplier B	1,811.47
Supplier C	1,996.18
Supplier D	140.26
Supplier E	5,400.00
Supplier F	1,387.65
Supplier G	895.52
Supplier H	1,369.92
Supplier I	772.10
Supplier J	1,642.50
Supplier K	1,849.89
Total	18,542.13

We can also see that the Balance Sheet includes 'Accounts Payable' of £18,542. The balance schedule entitled 'Creditors Control Account' on the right hand side (again, this has been extracted from the accounting system) shows a matching total balance.

But so what? A bunch of numbers agrees to another bunch of numbers. We could have fabricated this by entering the required numbers into the system just to make it balance, right?

If you take a closer look at the Schedule of cash balances on the right, you will see the second number down is £1,375.85. This is the balance of the bank account (known in the system as 'Current account 2'), which we reconciled to independent data in point 1. If you look at the Creditors Control Account below it, you will see the number £5,400 highlighted. Again, this is the balance of the supplier account we reconciled in point 1.

The point here is that every number in the balance schedule has been reconciled to independent data, so the balance schedules have been verified.

Naturally, as business owners, it's not your place to carry out these reconciliations, and I would reiterate once again that the point of this book is not to turn my readers into accountants. The point is that you should be able to ask your Finance Director, or Management Accountant, or external accountant, to show you the balance schedules or reconciliations for every number in your Management Accounts in order to prove that they have been compiled correctly.

Reporting - Relevance, Impartiality, Accuracy

The control mechanism for Reporting is actually broken into three standards:

- **Relevance** - There's no point reporting on statistics or figures which are not relevant to the business. But relevance can change over time. If the business model or product mix changes, certain metrics may no longer be relevant to the business, so there is little point in spending time reporting on them.
- **Impartiality** - Reports should contain data, statistics and figures, not opinions. The data should be presented in an impartial way, free from influence or agenda, so that the reports can be interpreted from different perspectives and discussed openly at board meetings.
- **Accuracy** - It goes without saying that reports should be accurate. Inaccurate reports are essentially worthless.

Once reports have been created, they should be reviewed frequently for the three factors above. Irrelevant reports should be amended or discontinued, care should be taken to avoid presenting biased reports and any inaccurate reporting should be reviewed to understand the reasons why, so that reporting processes can be amended.

External Factors - Weighted Sensitivity Metrics

The control mechanism for External Factors is the **Weighted Sensitivity Metrics** identified by the business as part of the fourth point of control.

These sensitivity metrics need to be reviewed on a regular basis, ideally as part of a monthly board meeting. The weighting is important and the most significant metrics should be given priority when assessing viability and actions.

Challenging What you See

As mentioned at the start of this chapter, Control Mechanisms can be used by Senior Management of the business to challenge the author of their financial reports, whether that's an external accountant or an internal Finance team. Challenging the data you are presented with is a vital part of taking your accountability seriously. I have seen businesses fail and the owner shrug and complain that the FD dropped the ball. Granted, he did drop the ball, but no one was there to pick it up because no one was checking that he was doing his job.

Challenging the numbers shouldn't be seen as confrontational or perceived as a lack of faith. Any competent Finance professional should welcome questions. Of course, the right approach is important but asking to see a reconciliation or a balance sheet schedule, or the rationale behind a report, so that you can verify the source data, is not only your right as senior manager or owner, it's also your obligation as a director.

Chapter 17 - Competence & Honesty

Sabotaging Your Work

It's crucial to recognise that there are ways your hard work can be undermined. As much as I have extolled the virtues of Management Accounts and pointed out the flawless reliability they provide, this only applies if incompetence, dishonesty and corruption can be eradicated.

Even the most robust of controls can be overridden if the person in charge of them makes a conscious decision to do so. The most frustrating part of this is that you can only do so much to guard against it. However, there are steps you can take to make incompetence and dishonesty less likely, or easier to detect.

Culture

Remember the quote we looked at in Chapter 5:

"If you want to build a ship, don't drum up people to collect wood and don't assign them tasks and work, but rather teach them to long for the endless immensity of the sea."

Antoine de Saint Exupéry
(French writer and aviator)

A collaborative and open culture will dramatically reduce the likelihood of any negative behaviours. A culture where people are constantly trying to hide problems or shift blame will encourage fearful conduct and a lack of accountability. This in turn will lead to dishonesty and deception.

By contrast, a regime where people have nothing to fear from making mistakes and are encouraged to be honest at all times will foster a positive and cooperative environment where everyone is working towards the same goal of establishing control and achieving profitable growth.

Incompetence

It's always difficult for a non-financial business owner or director to recruit a financial position and ensure that the person they have appointed has the required qualifications, experience and competence for the role.

Unfortunately, given the vast remit and potential requirements of a high-level finance role, there are no guarantees of competence, even if the person is fully qualified. Well-rounded experience should give you some reassurance but ultimately a highly experienced Finance Director will command a very high salary, so you may not have the budget to attract such a person.

Regardless of salary, the person you appoint will not know everything but may initially feel compelled to act as if they do. The key element in this situation is support. You need to create an environment where your Finance Director, or Finance Manager or Management Accountant, feels comfortable with being challenged and learns that they have nothing to fear from making a mistake. The best way to create this environment is regular but appropriate challenges. Asking them to show you their balance sheet schedules or bank reconciliations. Asking them why a particular number is so far over/under budget. Asking them why, how or when on a regular basis will show them that challenges will be coming their way, but that there is nothing to fear.

Of course you could take the view that you shouldn't have to treat them this way. After all, they're a well-paid and qualified member of staff and shouldn't need to be handled with kid gloves. Of course that's your call, but I've seen that approach in action and it culminated in bankruptcy and administrators, so I would suggest the collaborative and supportive approach works better.

If you use an external accountant, you are not immune from the incompetence effect. I have had several clients who have used external accountants and seen staggering examples of incompetence and malpractice. In my experience it's far more rare, as they have access to wider pools of talent and usually have multiple colleagues in the same practice who can get involved if necessary. However, they also have a vested interest in obfuscation and covering up errors if they can get away with it, and I have seen this happen too. Again the best approach is to educate yourself on the concepts, techniques and processes outlined in this book, so that you can investigate and challenge anything that doesn't look right, and hold whoever does your finances accountable.

Dishonesty

Dishonesty is not necessarily lying. It could just be the deliberate failure to clarify a misconception. It could be choosing not to disclose something because you know it would be received badly and you don't want to deal with the fallout.

Once again it comes down to culture. If you have created an environment in which people are comfortable enough to be honest, they will usually have no problem clarifying misconceptions and being straight with you.

Corruption and Fraud

This is the big one. Incompetence and dishonesty can be damaging and disappointing, but outright and wilful corruption can be utterly devastating. In this case your Finance Director or external accountant (it's rare, but it does happen) has deliberately and intentionally deceived you in order to achieve some kind of financial gain for themselves.

This can take many forms, such as colluding with a supplier to inflate invoices, fabricating financial documents to facilitate payment or outright lying to defraud the company in a multitude of ways.

Unfortunately, this can be difficult to detect. In the case of incompetence or casual dishonesty, there will usually be 'breadcrumbs' to give things away. When it comes to deliberate corruption, tracks are usually covered and key signs will be hidden as much as possible.

The best way to guard against corruption is to embrace the concepts and controls outlined in this book. If you understand how the reports are put together, where the numbers come from and use the control mechanisms described in the previous chapter to ensure that all your reports are reconciled to independent data, it will be very difficult for corruption to slip through the net.

Take Control

As you can see from this chapter, the key elements that contribute to the prevention of incompetence and dishonesty are as follows:

1. **Culture** - Creating a culture where your employees are comfortable with being challenged and have no fear of delivering bad news will encourage honesty and collaboration.
2. **Education** - Understanding the concepts and techniques outlined in this book will enable you to read financial reports and hold your finance team (whether internal or external) to account.

Chapter 18 - Ongoing Controls

Ongoing Controls

There are four areas (apart from the ongoing execution of Management Accounts and supporting reports) that will need constant attention if control is to be maintained to the maximum extent possible

1. Relevance of Reporting - Reports should be periodically reviewed to make sure the subject matter is still relevant. Irrelevant reports should be discontinued or amended as appropriate.
2. Reviews of Weighted Sensitivity Metrics - Reviewing your risk register is an important monthly task. Sensitivity metrics should be monitored regularly and acceptable levels should be defined. For example, if the USD exchange rate drops below 1.2, we need to formulate a hedging strategy. New risks should be identified and added to the register, risks which no longer apply should be removed.
3. Scanning the Horizon - Upcoming events should be identified and assessed as they occur and added to your risk register if deemed a potential threat.
4. Continuous Improvement - This is a broad term, but any opportunity to improve your control measures should be seized.

These items should all have review dates and accountability should be assigned to specific people.

Chronological and Perpetual

Always remember two things when it comes to the Control Cycle.

1. It is **chronological** - You must carry out Performance Evaluation for each period (month) before assessing your Economic Viability or worrying about your Compliance.
2. It is **perpetual** - You will never achieve full and complete control of your business. Even if you somehow achieve this miracle in one month, you will have to start all over again the following month.

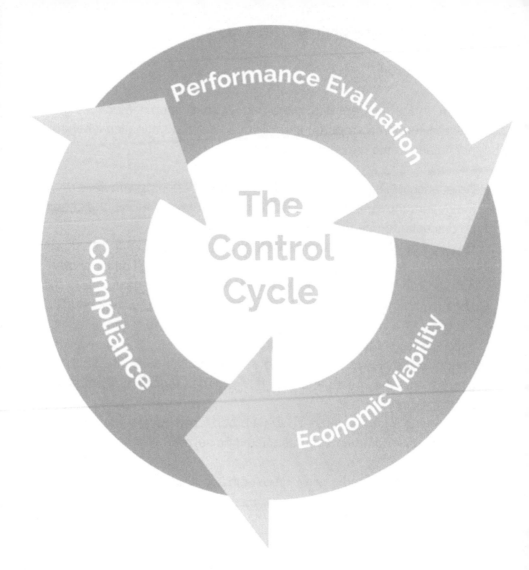

Don't Leave it to Chance

Hopefully, by this point of the book (ie the end), you have seen or learned something you didn't already know. If you are still wondering why you need a budget or why you need to fulfil the three Elements of Control, then I would suggest re-reading the book more carefully. All businesses will benefit from the processes and strategies outlined in this book. Failing businesses can be turned around, successful businesses can maximise that success and business owners can finally realise the objectives they had in mind when setting out on their journey.

I have spent my career working in and with businesses who were rudderless and devoid of any deliberate strategy. Several of these companies have been successful, some of them enormously so, but this has been more by accident than by design. They have relied heavily on the quality of their product and benefited from a healthy dose of luck in order to become successful. Even then, at the peak of their success, they have no idea where they're going or what the long term goal is.

Similarly, I have worked with many businesses who have not been so successful and, unfortunately, a few who have failed completely.

Something many of these businesses had in common is a lack of strategy and a lack of control. Without strategy to determine the direction of your business and control to ensure you're following that strategy, too much is left to chance and fortunes can change overnight.

This book doesn't give you all the answers, but it sets you on the path. With a bit of research, support from your network and colleagues (and from me if you reach out) you can take what you've learned from this book to the next level and truly take control of the future of your business.

If you need further guidance on anything you have read in this book, please contact PPX Consulting via our website.